FOR ORGANS, PIANOS & ELECTRONIC KEYBOARDS

E-Z PLAY® TODAY

162

The **Lounge Music COLLECTION**

ISBN 0-7935-8231-8

7777 W. BLUEMOUND RD. P.O. BOX 13819 MILWAUKEE, WI 53213

Visit Hal Leonard Online at
www.halleonard.com

Contents

Alfie
Theme from the Paramount Picture ALFIE

Registration 9
Rhythm: 8 Beat or Pops

Words by Hal David
Music by Burt Bacharach

Beyond the Sea

Registration 7
Rhythm: Slow Rock or Ballad

English Lyrics by Jack Lawrence
Music and French Lyrics by Charles Trenet

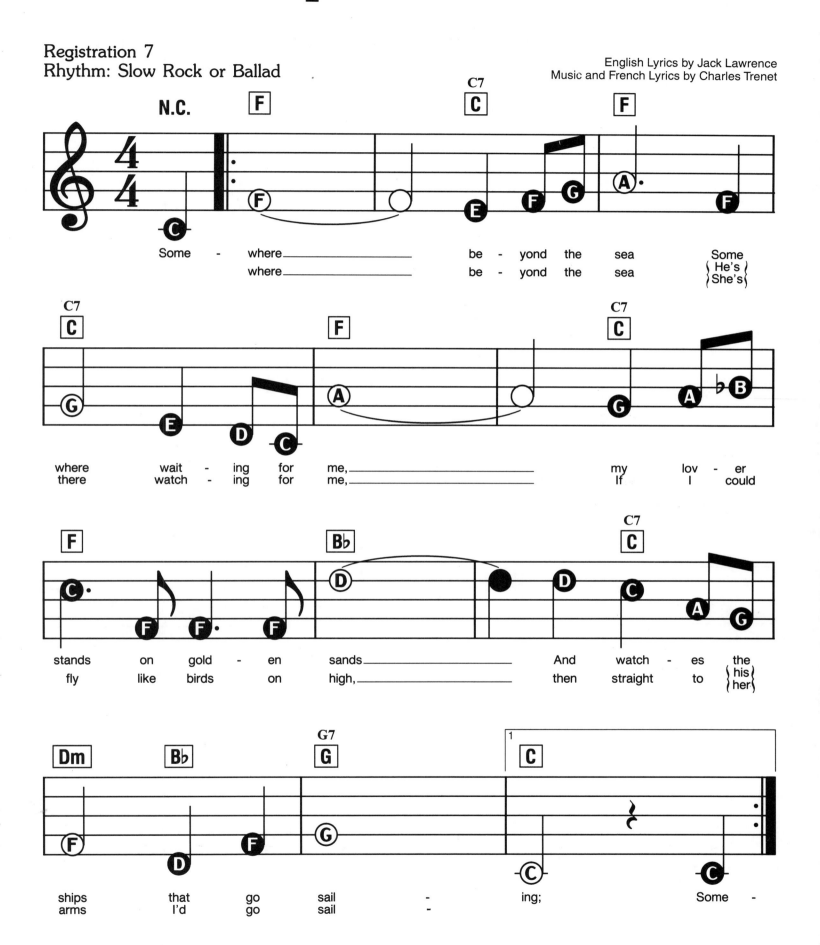

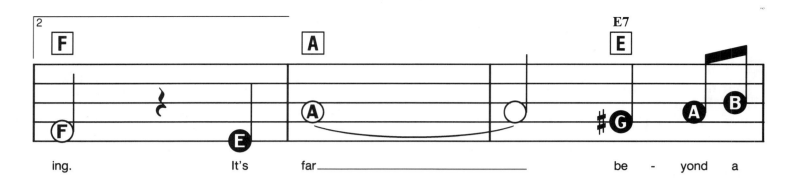

ing. It's far_____ be - yond a

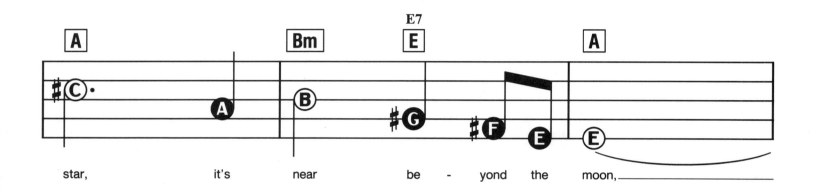

star, it's near be - yond the moon,_____

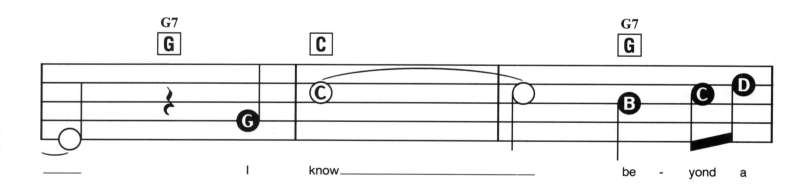

___ I know_____ be - yond a

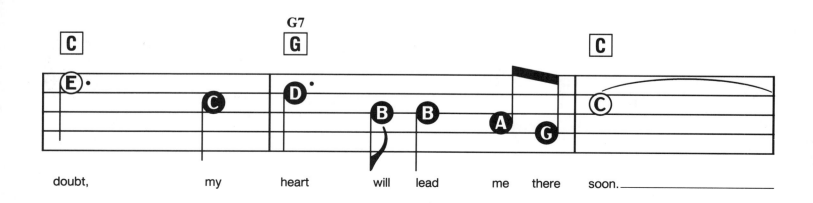

doubt, my heart will lead me there soon._____

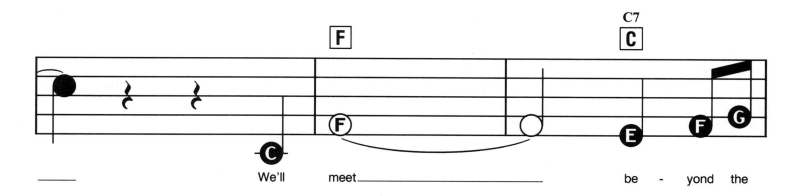

We'll meet _____ be - yond the

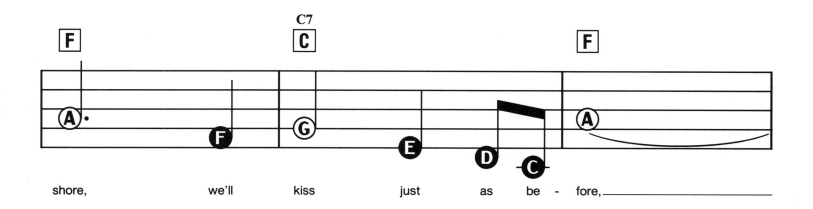

shore, we'll kiss just as be - fore, _____

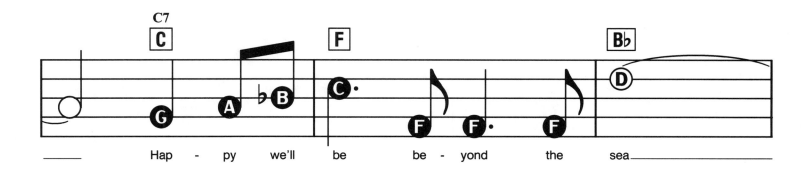

_____ Hap - py we'll be be - yond the sea _____

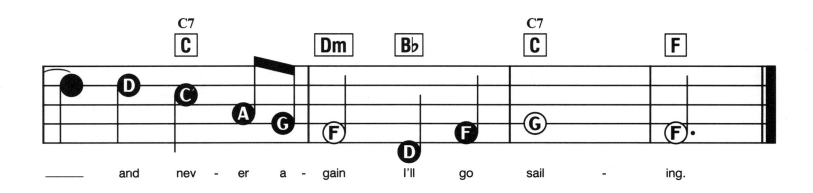

_____ and nev - er a - gain I'll go sail - ing.

Autumn Leaves
(Les Feuilles Mortes)

Registration 2
Rhythm: Fox Trot or Swing

English lyric by Johnny Mercer
French lyric by Jacques Prevert
Music by Joseph Kosma

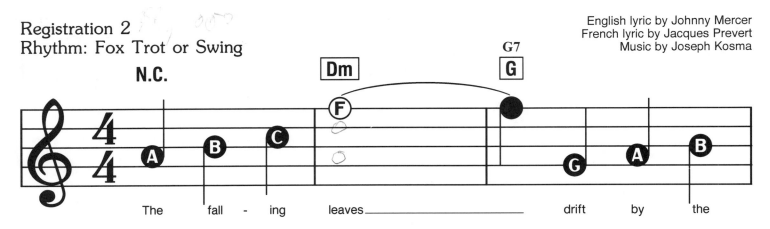

The fall - ing leaves _____ drift by the

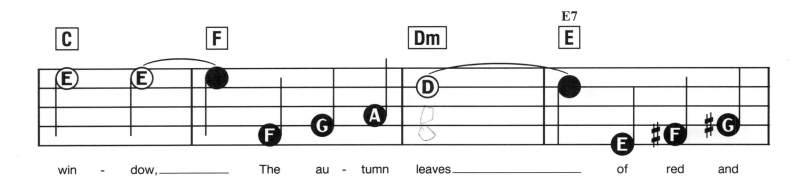

win - dow, _____ The au - tumn leaves _____ of red and

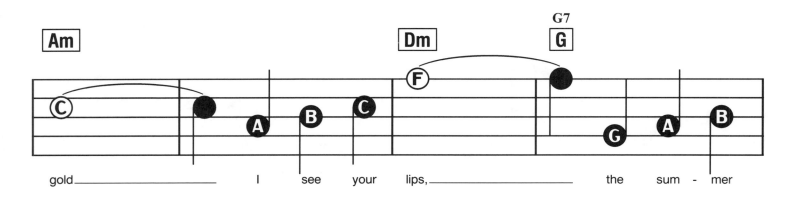

gold _____ I see your lips, _____ the sum - mer

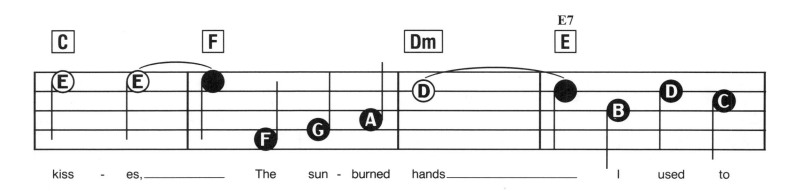

kiss - es, _____ The sun - burned hands _____ I used to

11

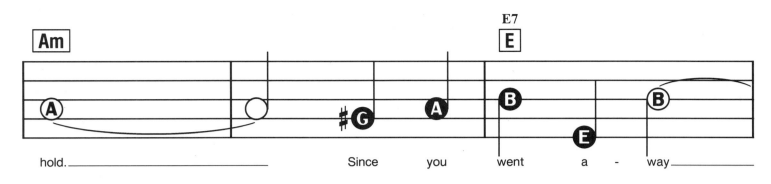

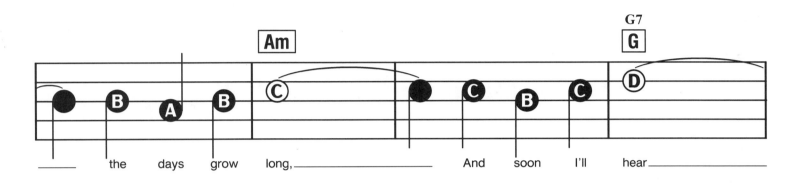

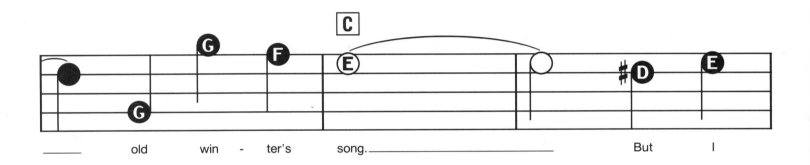

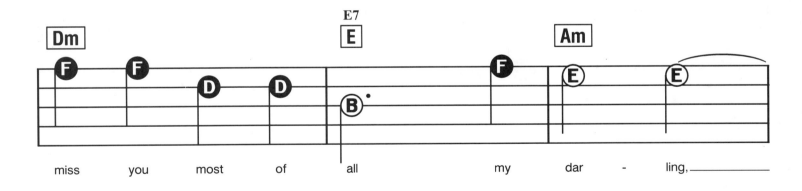

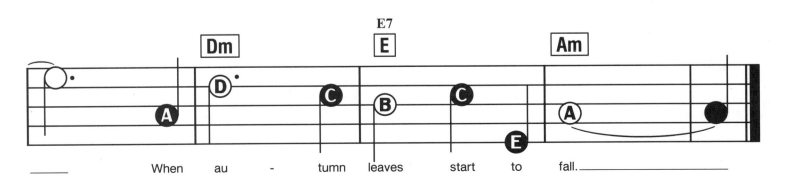

Born Free

Registration 4
Rhythm: Ballad

Words by Don Black
Music by John Barry

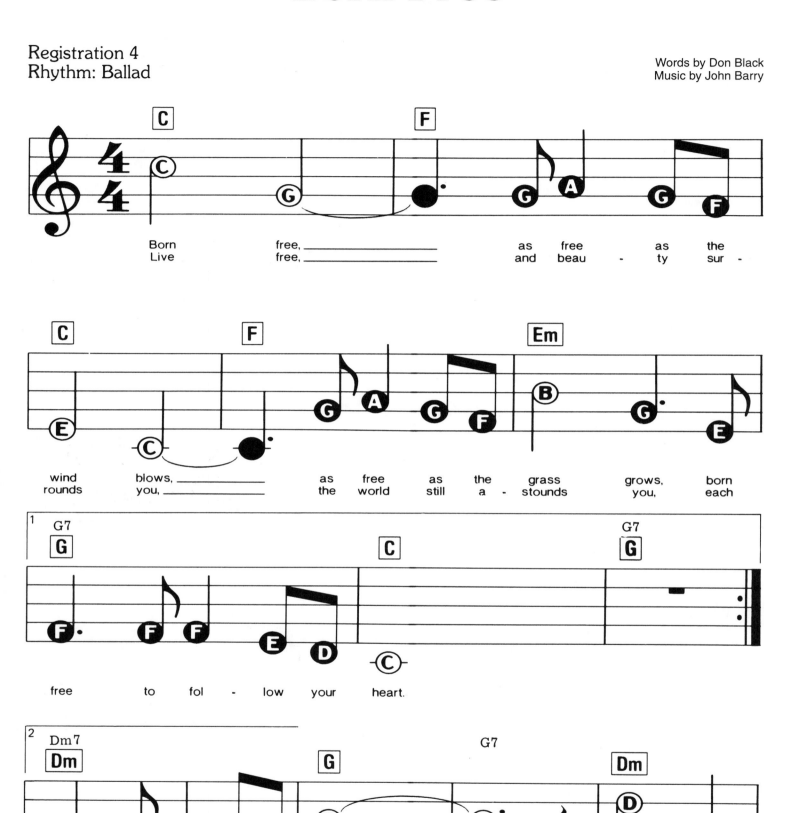

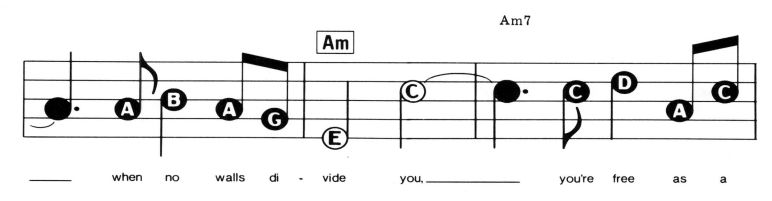

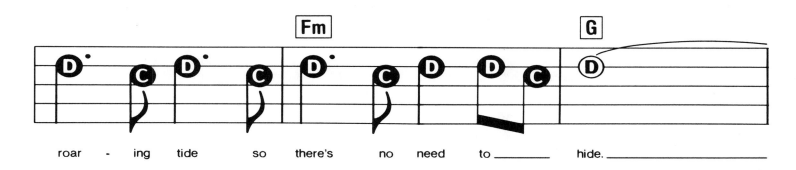

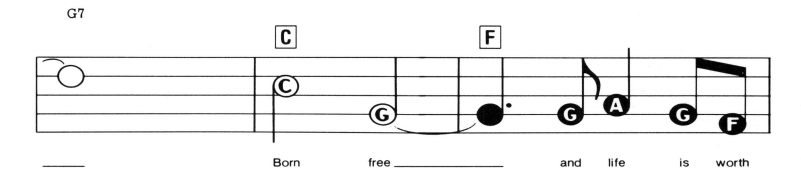

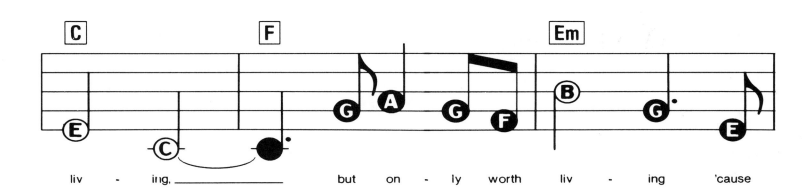

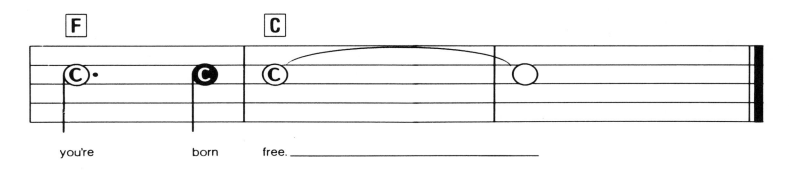

Call Me

Registration 7
Rhythm: Rock or 8 Beat

Words and Music by
Tony Hatch

MCA music publishing

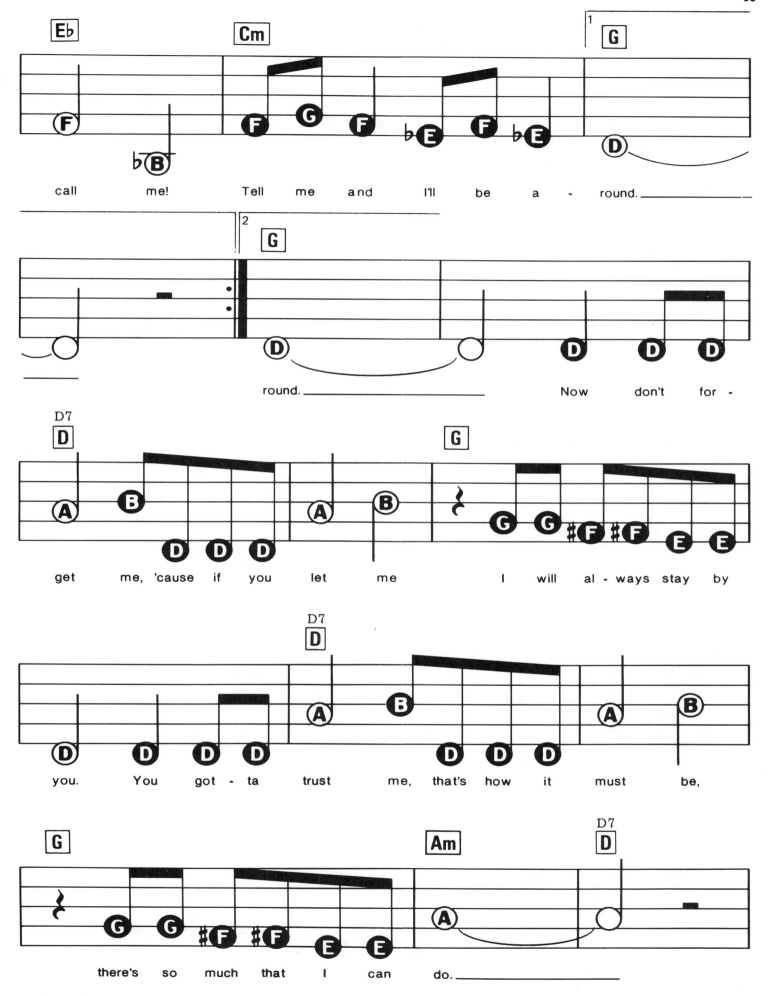

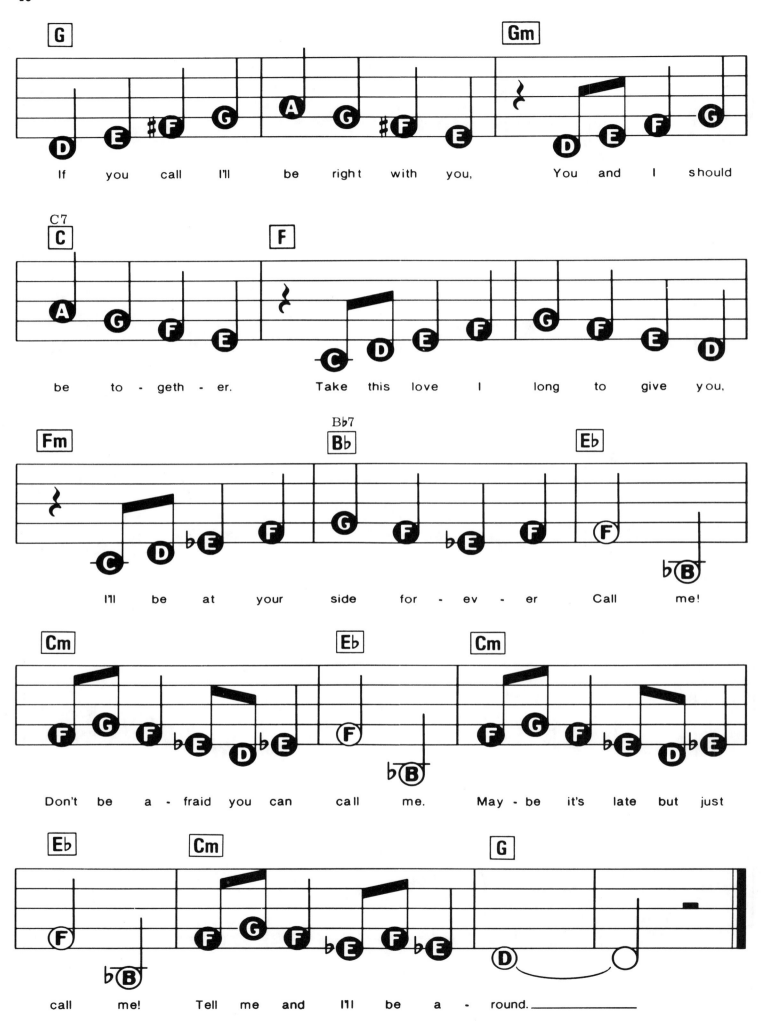

(They Long to Be)
Close to You

Registration 2
Rhythm: Slow Rock

Lyric by Hal David
Music by Burt Bacharach

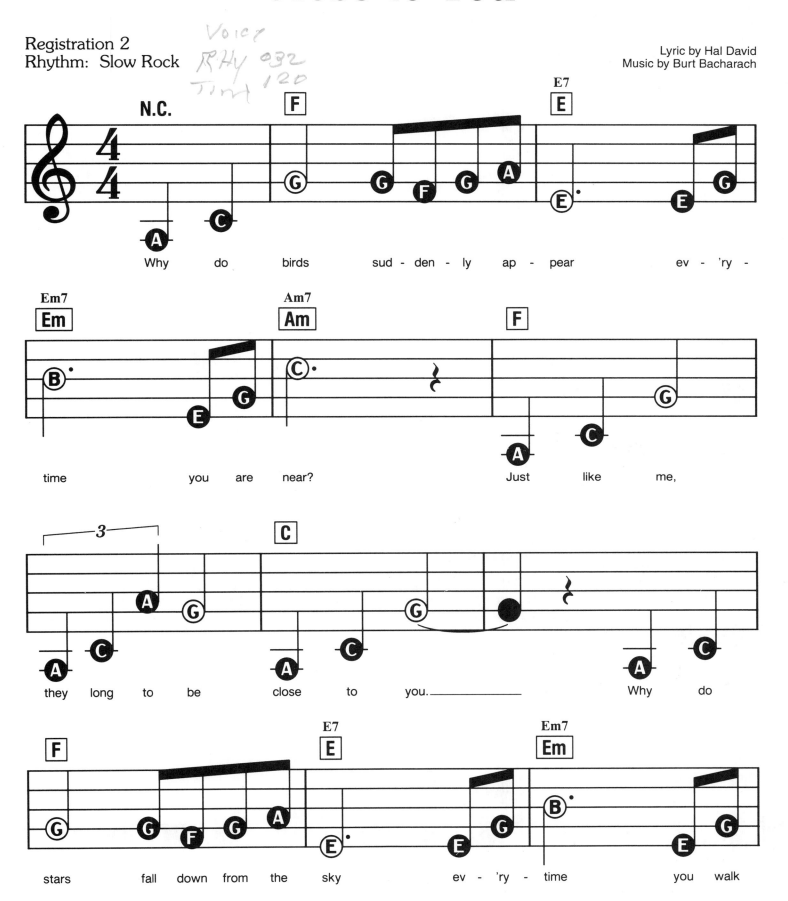

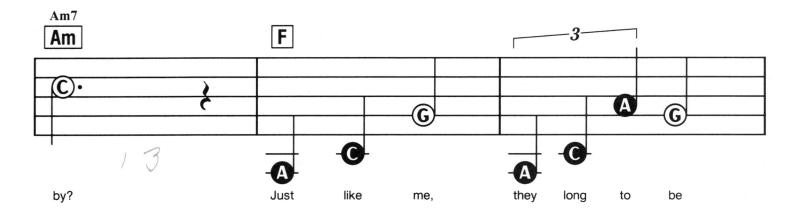

by? Just like me, they long to be

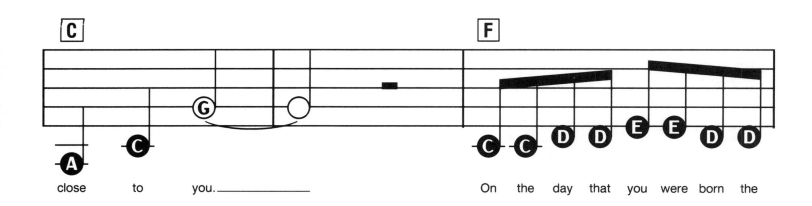

close to you._____ On the day that you were born the

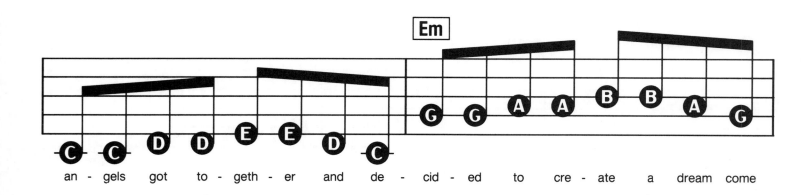

an - gels got to - geth - er and de - cid - ed to cre - ate a dream come

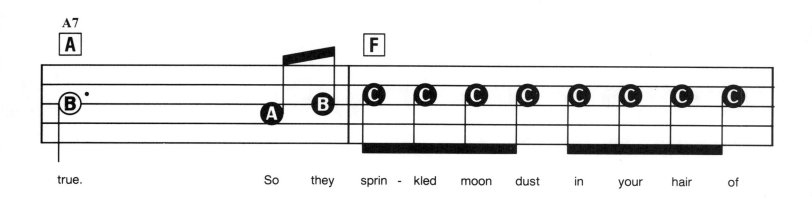

true. So they sprin - kled moon dust in your hair of

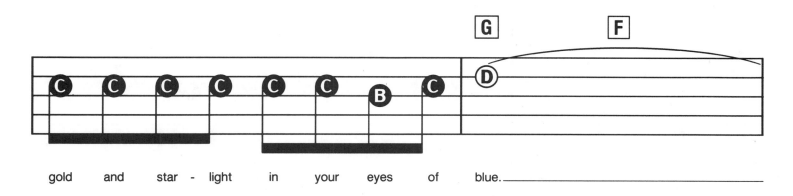

gold and star - light in your eyes of blue._____

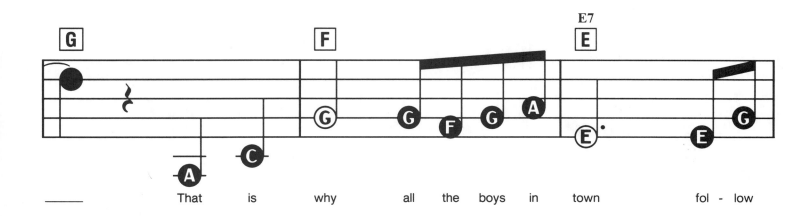

_____ That is why all the boys in town fol - low

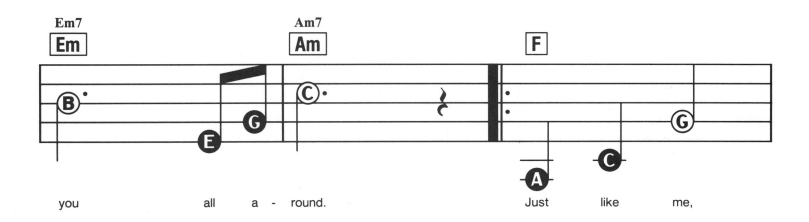

you all a - round. Just like me,

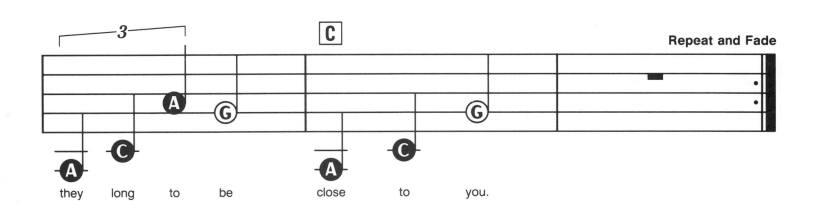

they long to be close to you.

Call Me Irresponsible

from the Paramount Picture PAPA'S DELICATE CONDITION

Registration 8
Rhythm: Swing

Words by Sammy Cahn
Music by James Van Heusen

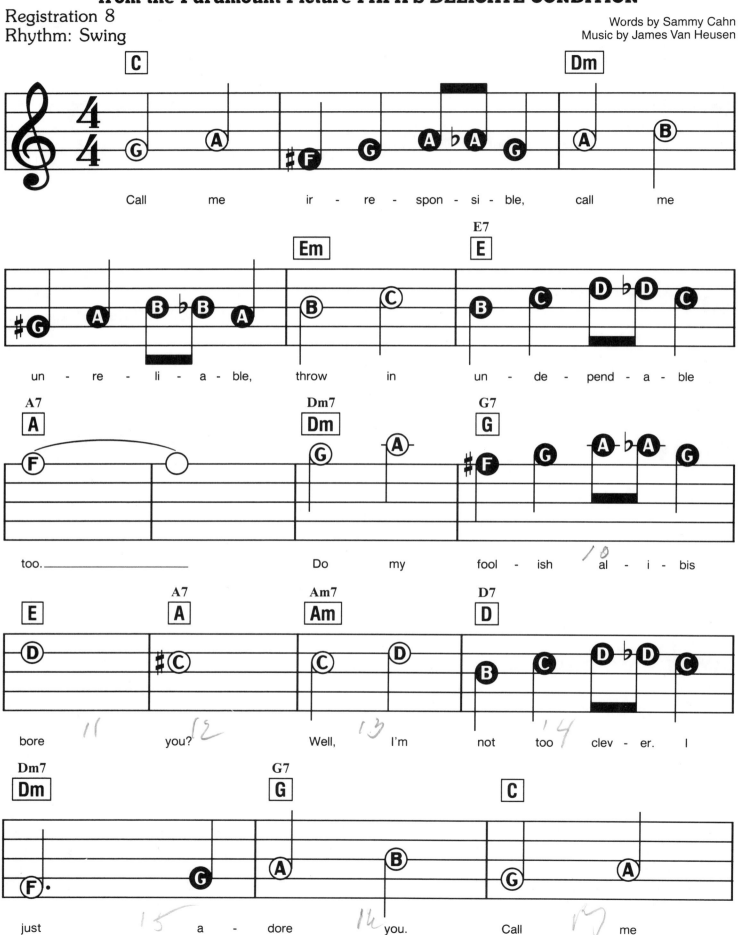

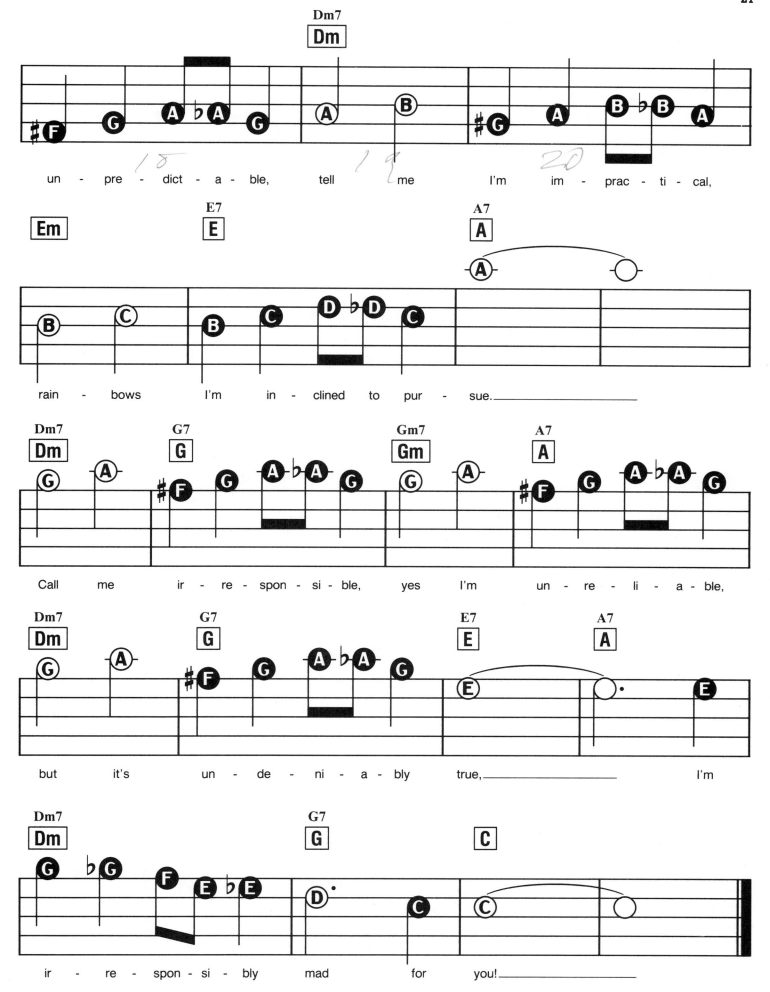

Copacabana
(At the Copa)

Registration 1
Rhythm: Disco

Words by Bruce Sussman and Jack Feldman
Music by Barry Manilow

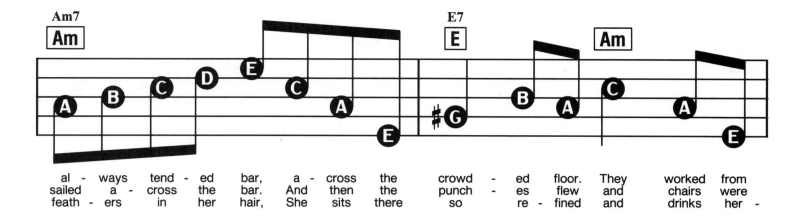

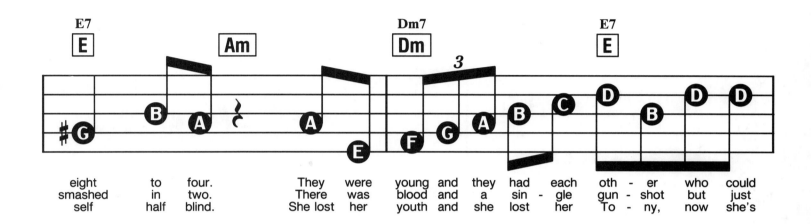

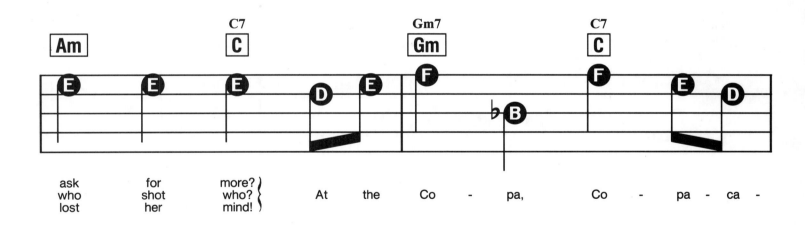

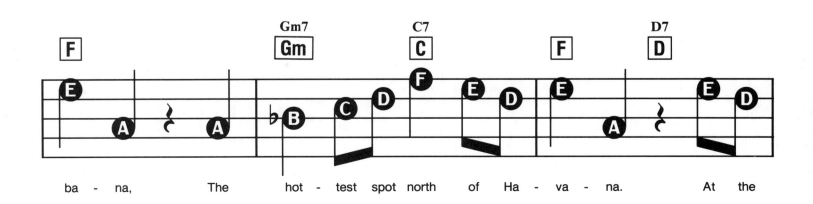

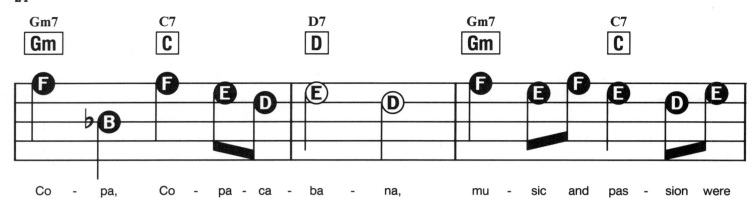

Co - pa, Co - pa - ca - ba - na, mu - sic and pas - sion were

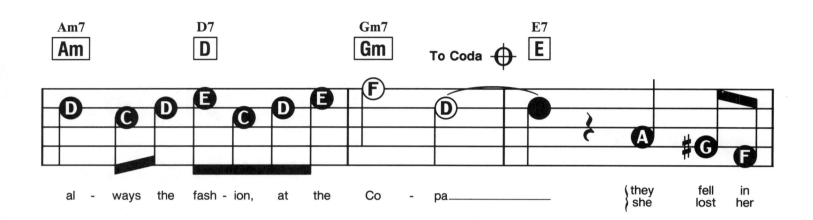

al - ways the fash - ion, at the Co - pa_____ { they fell in
{ she lost her

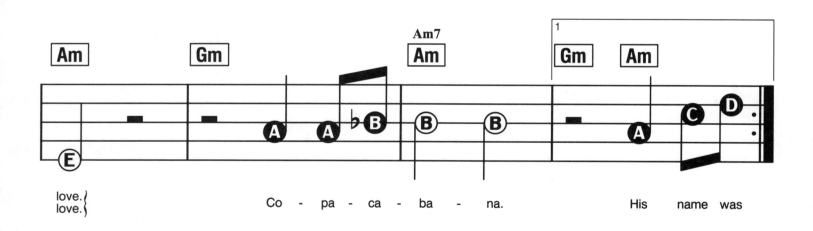

love. {
love. {
Co - pa - ca - ba - na. His name was

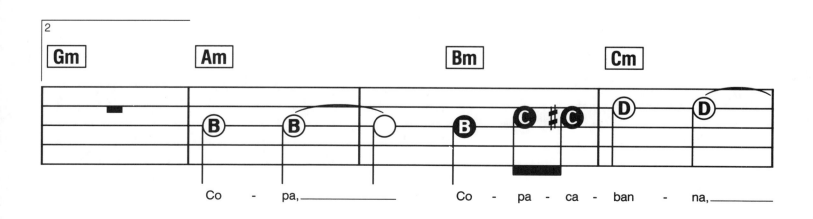

Co - pa,_____ Co - pa - ca - ban - na,_____

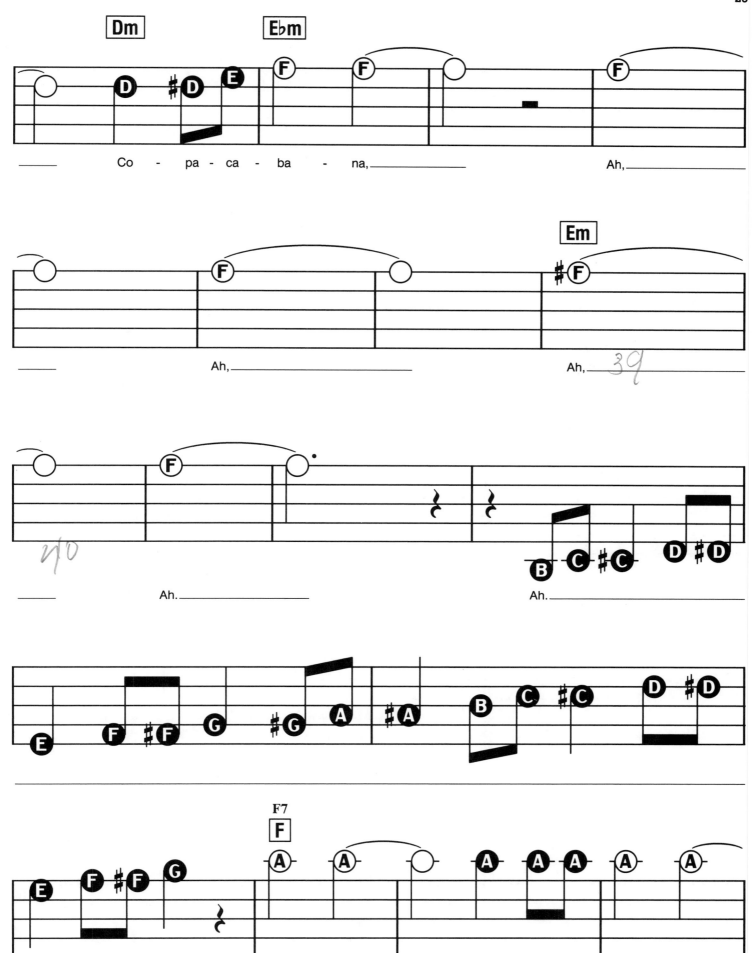

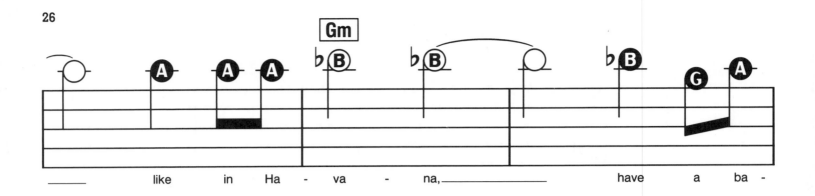

like in Ha - va - na,_____ have a ba -

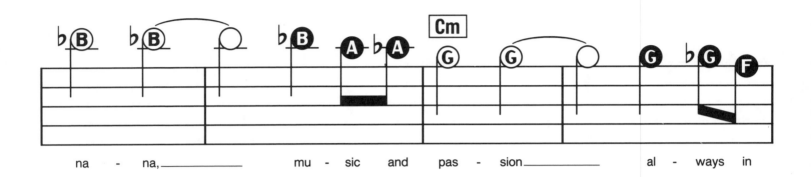

na - na,_____ mu - sic and pas - sion_____ al - ways in

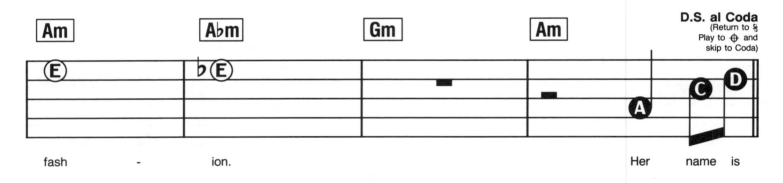

fash - ion. Her name is

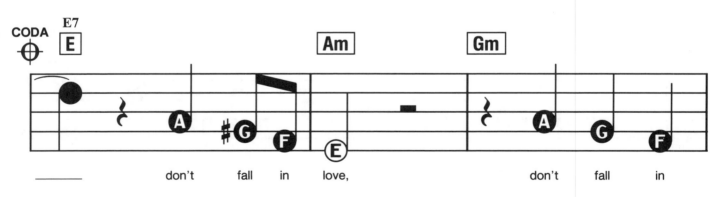

_____ don't fall in love, don't fall in

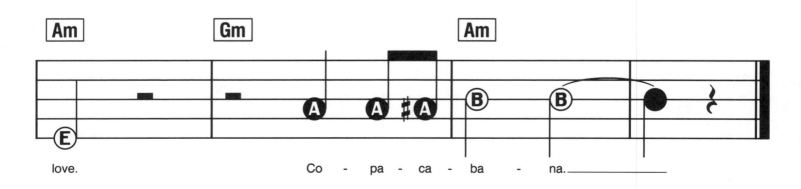

love. Co - pa - ca - ba - na._____

Feelings
(¿Dime?)

Registration 5
Rhythm: Slow Rock

English Words and Music by Morris Albert
Spanish lyric by Thomas Fundora

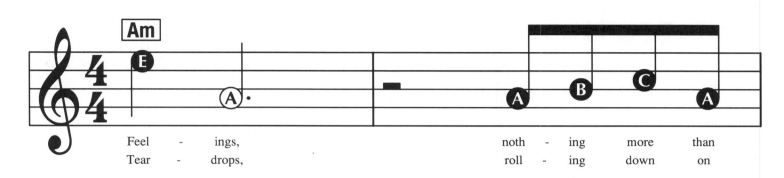

Feel - ings,   noth - ing more than
Tear - drops,   roll - ing down on

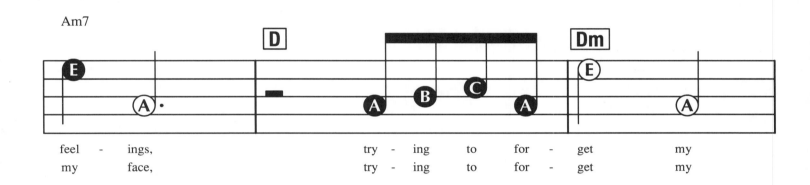

feel - ings,   try - ing to for - get my
my face,   try - ing to for - get my

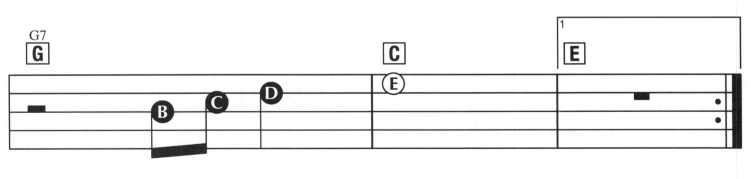

feel - ings of   love.
feel - ings of   love.

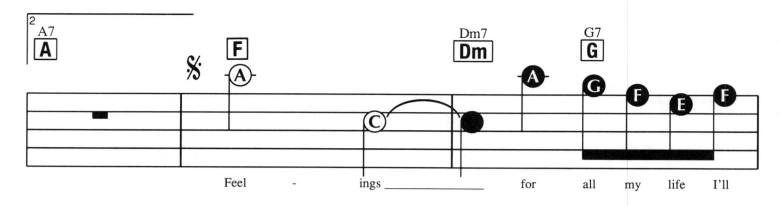

Feel - ings _____ for all my life I'll

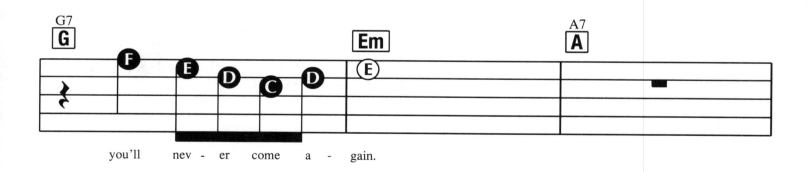

feel it. I wish I nev - er met you, girl;

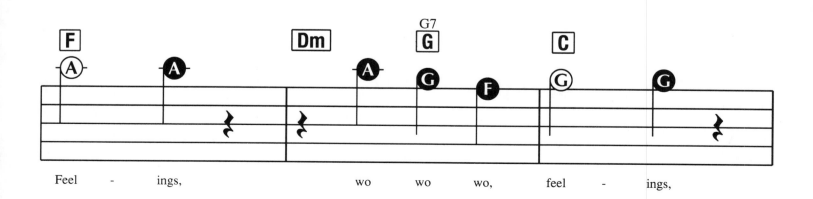

you'll nev - er come a - gain.

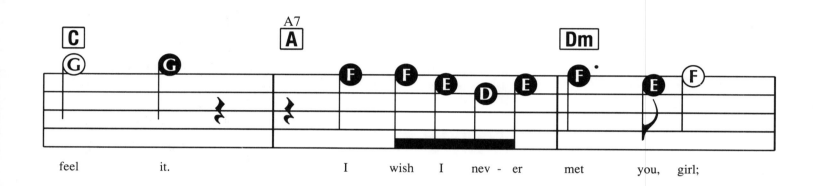

Feel - ings, wo wo wo, feel - ings,

29

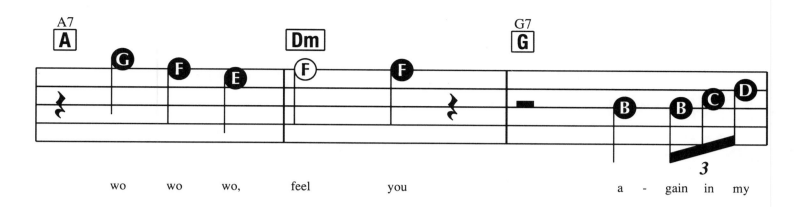

wo wo wo, feel you a - gain in my

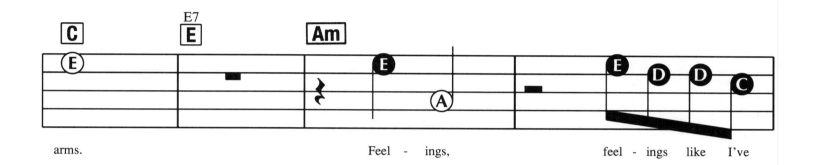

arms. Feel - ings, feel - ings like I've

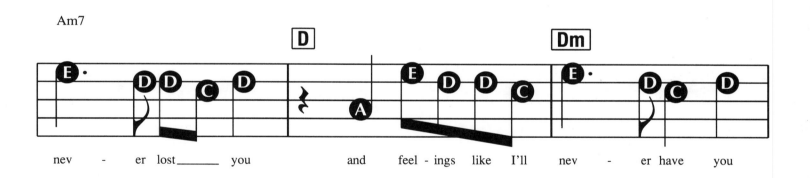

nev - er lost_____ you and feel - ings like I'll nev - er have you

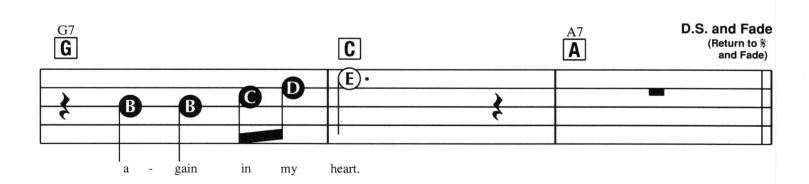

D.S. and Fade
(Return to 𝄋 and Fade)

a - gain in my heart.

Danke Schoen

Registration 9
Rhythm: Swing

Lyrics by Kurt Schwabach and Milt Gabler
Music by Bert Kaempfert

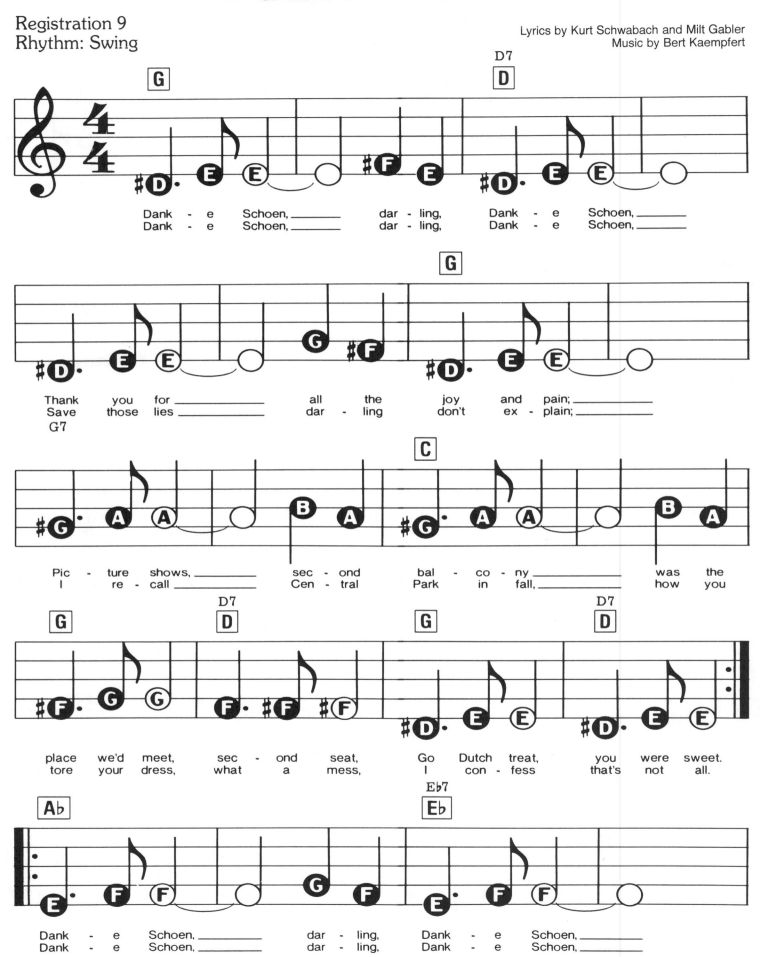

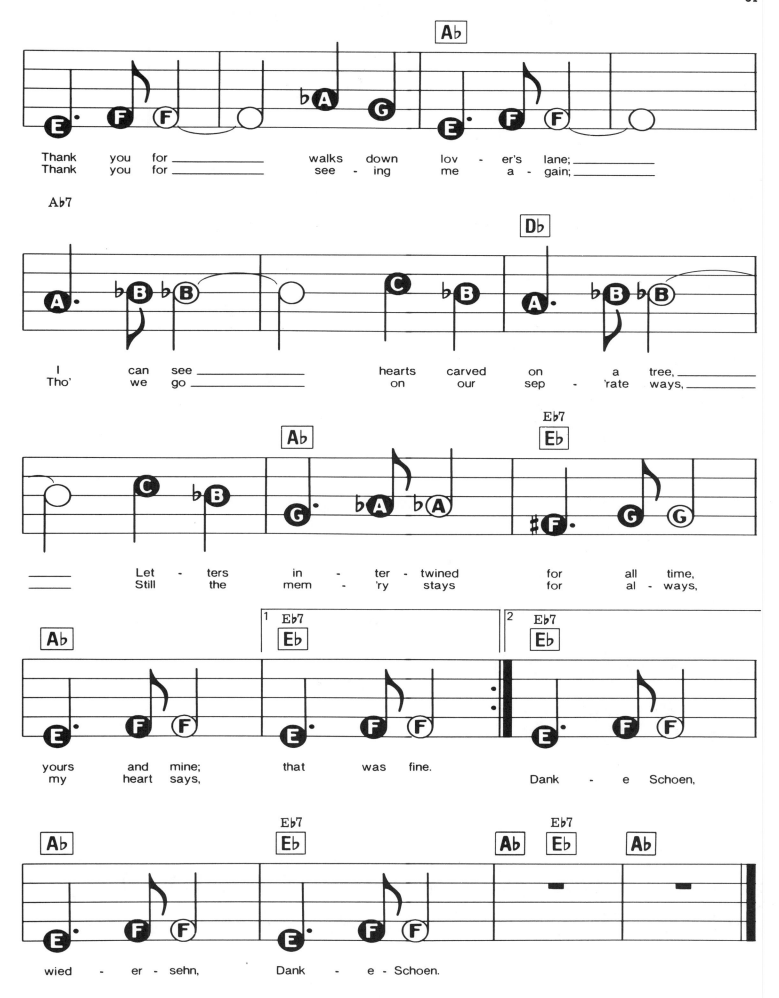

Don't Cry for Me Argentina
from EVITA

Registration 9
Rhythm: Tango or Latin

Words by Tim Rice
Music by Andrew Lloyd Webber

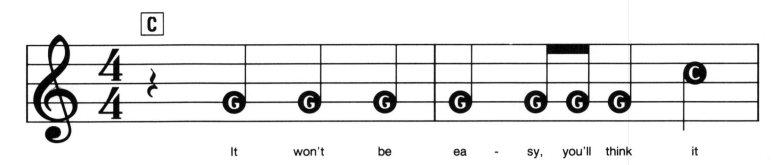

It won't be ea - sy, you'll think it

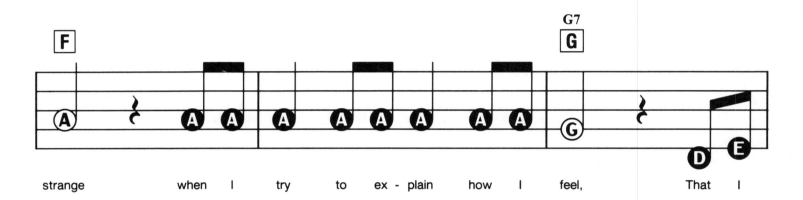

strange when I try to ex - plain how I feel, That I

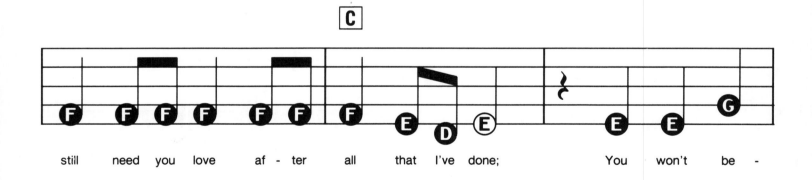

still need you love af - ter all that I've done; You won't be -

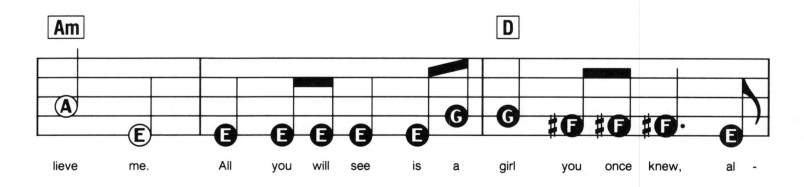

lieve me. All you will see is a girl you once knew, al -

MCA music publishing

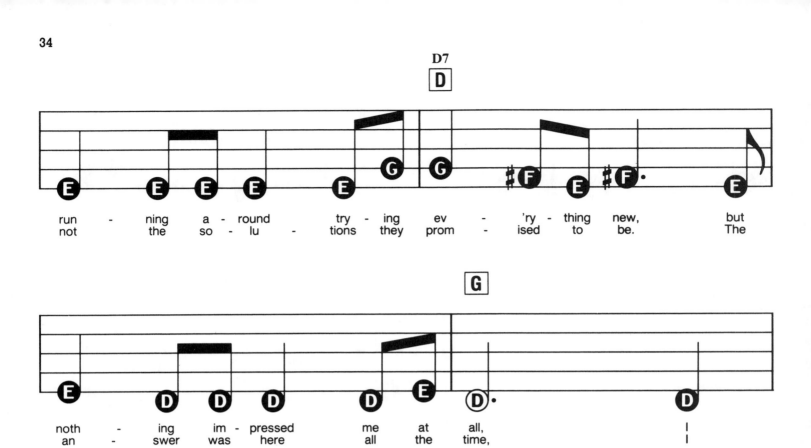

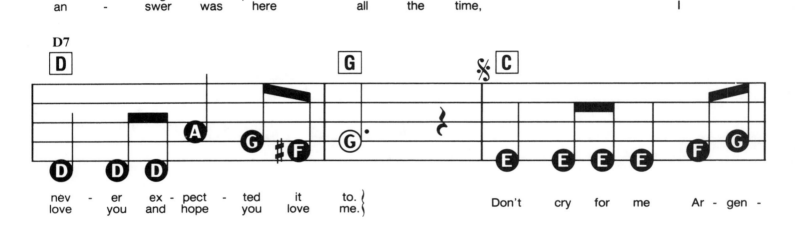

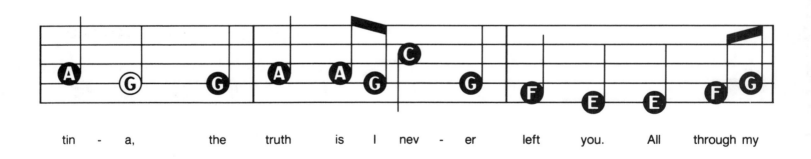

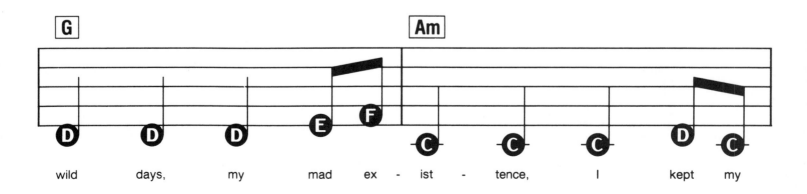

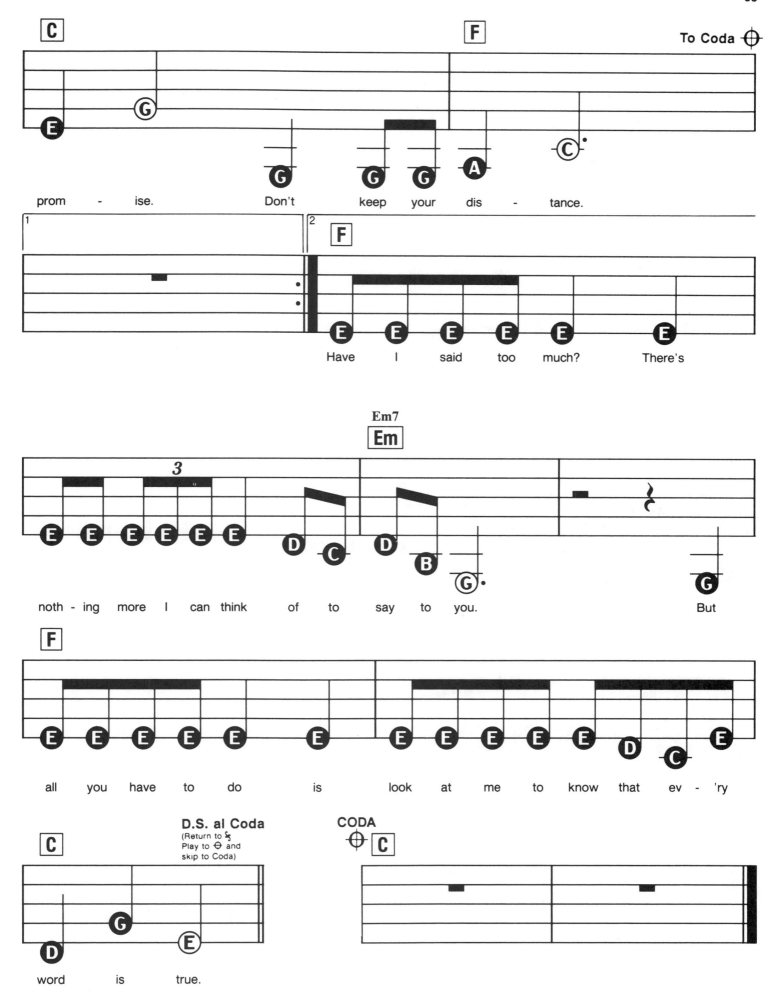

Fever

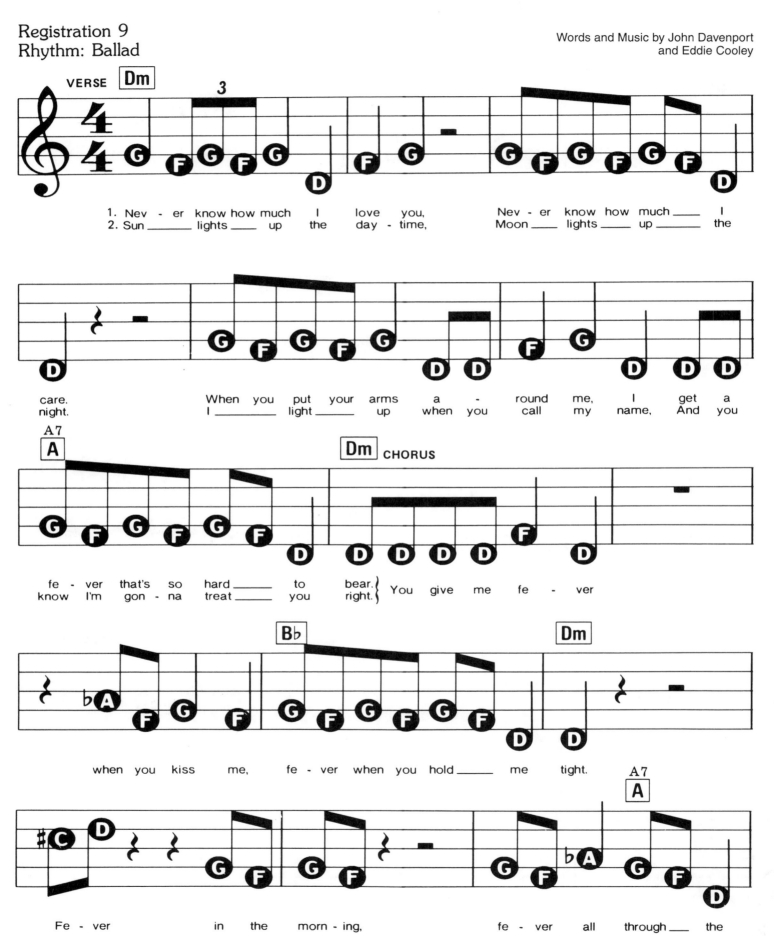

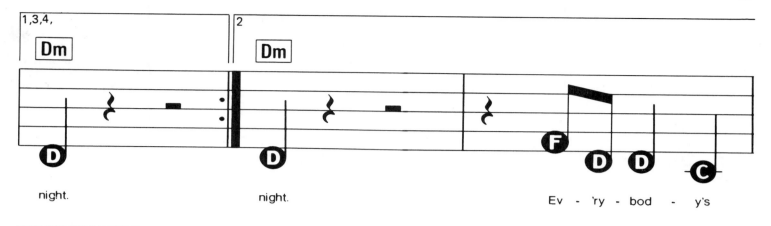

night.　　　　night.　　　　Ev - 'ry - bod - y's

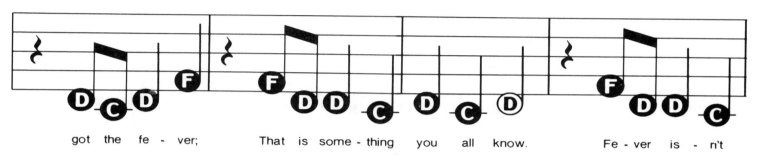

got the fe - ver;　That is some - thing you all know.　Fe - ver is - n't

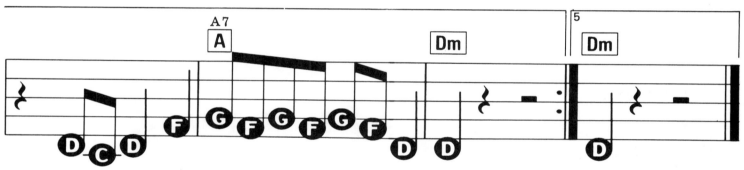

such a new thing, Fe - ver start - ed long ____ a - go.　　burn.

Additional Verses

Verse 3
Romeo loved Juliet,
Juliet she felt the same.
When he put his arms around her, he said,
"Julie, baby, you're my flame."

Chorus:
Thou givest fever, when we kisseth,
FEVER with thy flaming youth.
FEVER — I'm afire,
FEVER, yea I burn forsooth.

Verse 4
Captain Smith and Pocahantas
Had a very mad affair,
When her Daddy tried to kill him, she said,
"Daddy-o don't you dare."

Chorus:
Give me fever, with his kisses,
FEVER when he holds me tight.
FEVER — I'm his Missus,
Oh Daddy won't you treat him right.

Verse 5
Now you've listened to my story
Here's the point that I have made.
Chicks were born to give you FEVER
Be it fahrenheit or centigrade.

Chorus:
They give you FEVER, when you kiss them,
FEVER if you live and learn.
FEVER — till you sizzle,
What a lovely way to burn.

The Girl from Ipanema
(Garôta De Ipanema)

English Words by Norman Gimbel
Original Words by Vinicius de Moraes
Music by Antonio Carlos Jobim

Registration 4
Rhythm: Latin or Bossa Nova

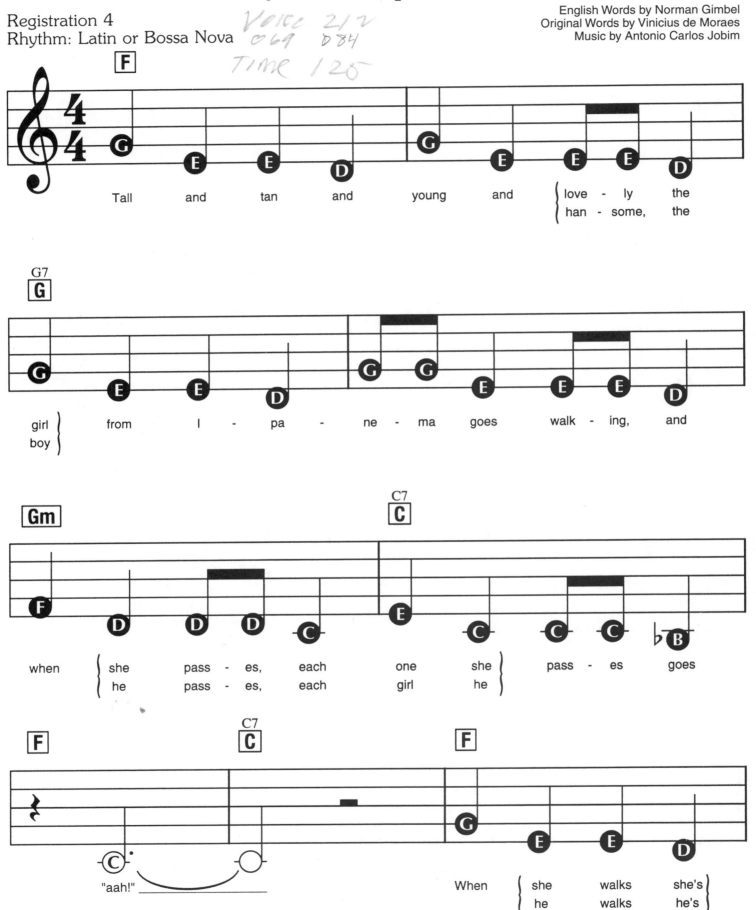

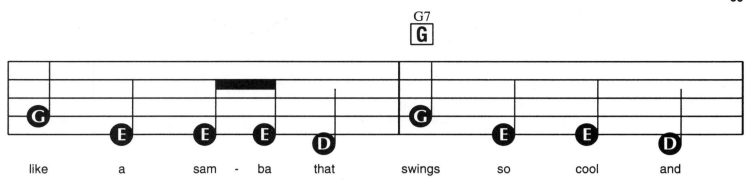

like a sam - ba that swings so cool and

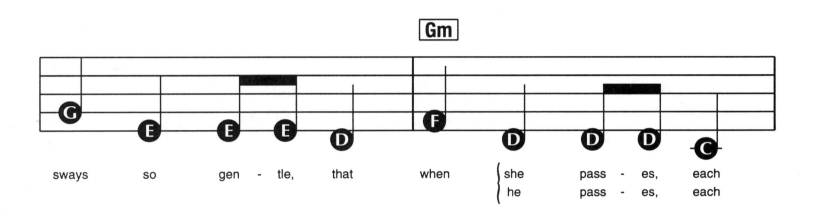

sways so gen - tle, that when {she / he} pass - es, each

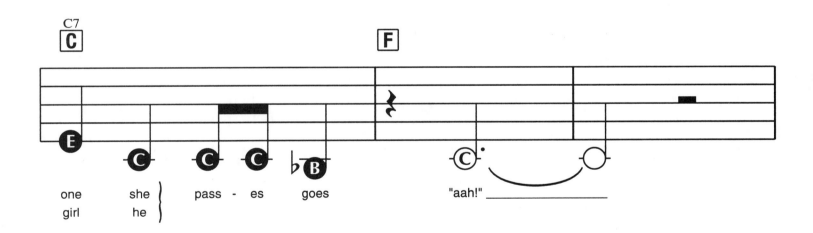

{one she / girl he} pass - es goes "aah!" _____

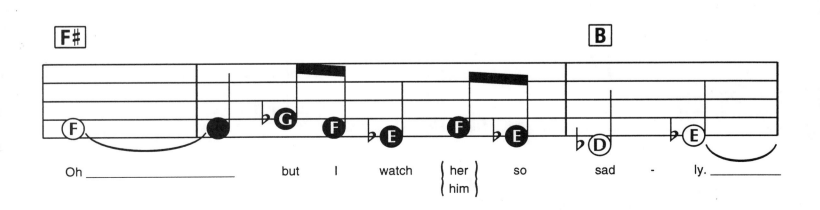

Oh _____ but I watch {her / him} so sad - ly. _____

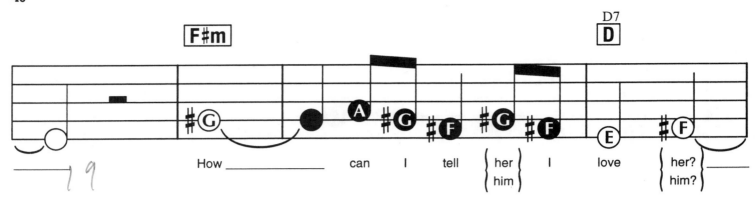

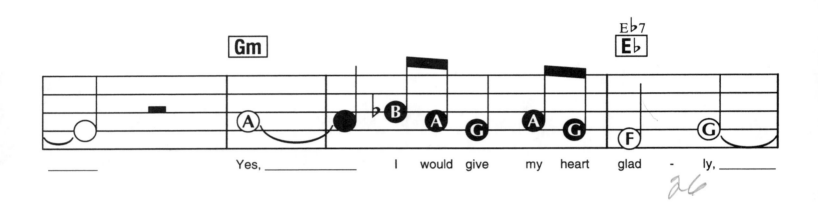

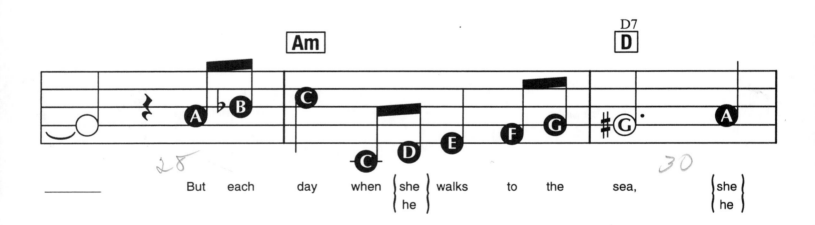

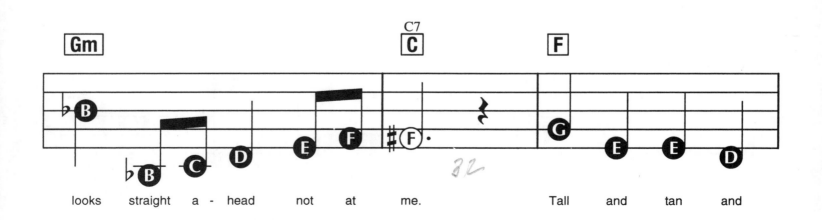

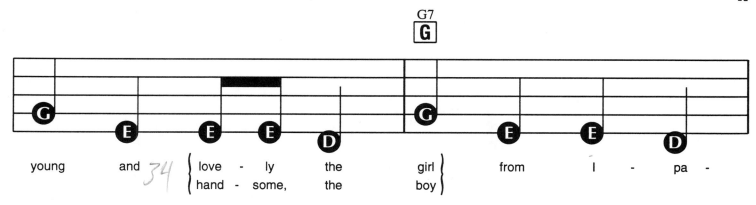

young and 34 {love - ly the girl} from I - pa -
{hand - some, the boy}

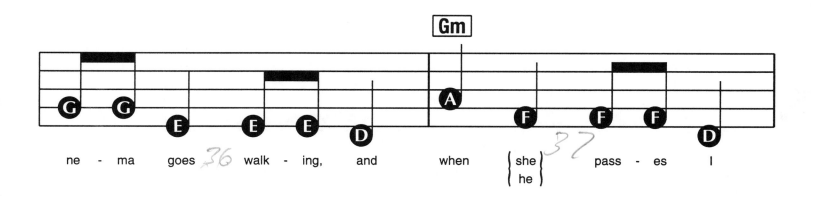

ne - ma goes 36 walk - ing, and when {she} 37 pass - es I
{he}

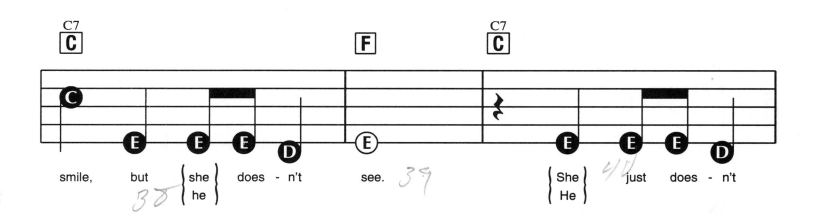

smile, but 38 {she} does - n't see. 39 {She} 40 just does - n't
{he} {He}

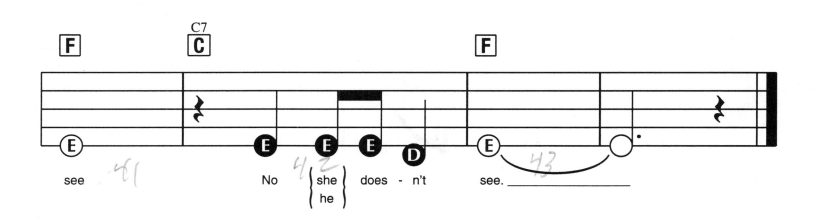

see 41 No 42 {she} does - n't see. 43
{he}

Girl Talk
from the Paramount Picture HARLOW

Registration 1
Rhythm: Swing or Shuffle

Words by Bobby Troup
Music by Neal Hefti

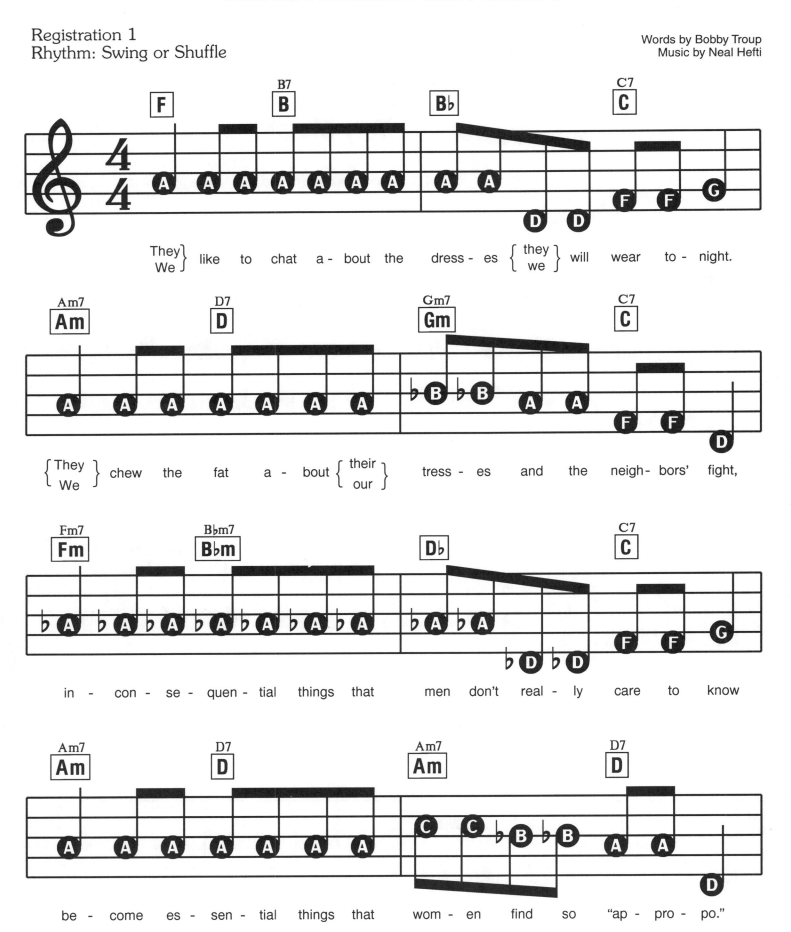

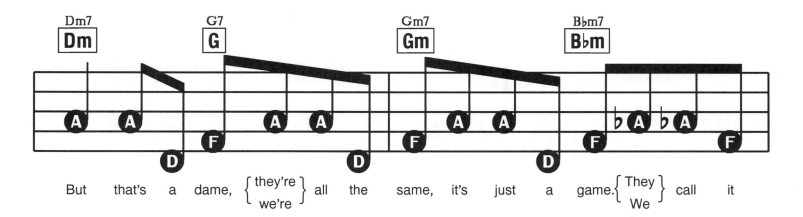

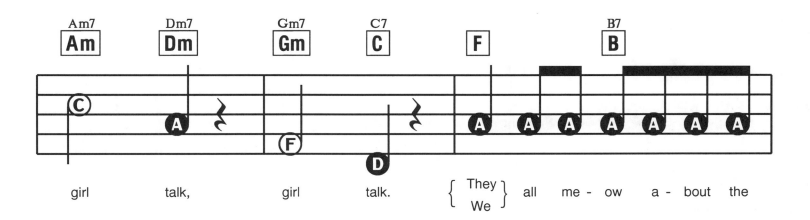

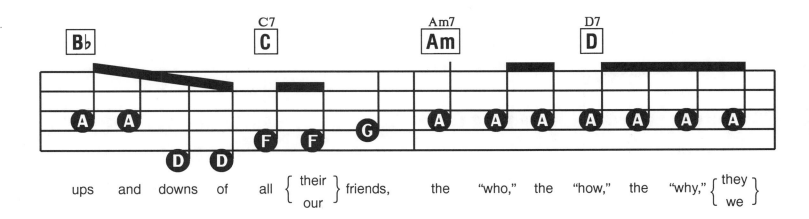

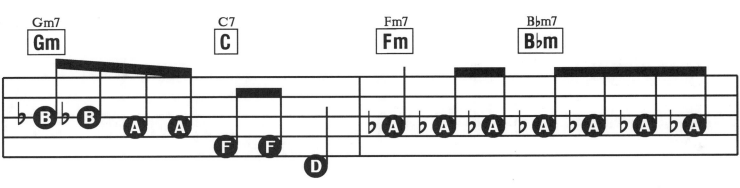

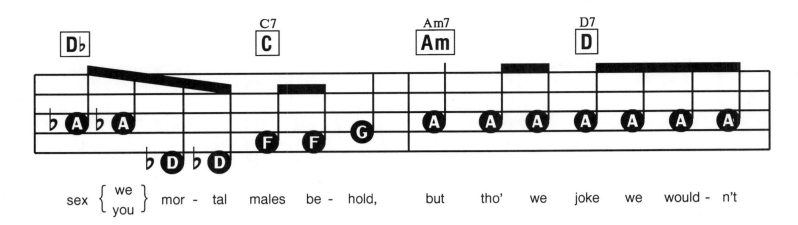

sex { we / you } mor - tal males be - hold, but tho' we joke we would - n't

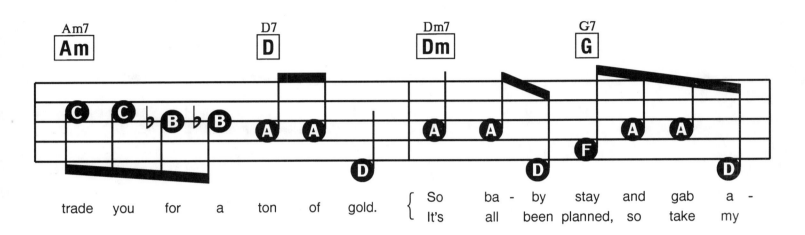

trade you for a ton of gold. { So ba - by stay and gab a - / It's all been planned, so take my

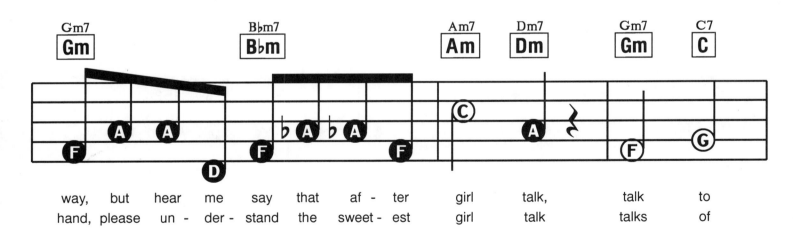

way, but hear me say that af - ter girl talk, talk to
hand, please un - der - stand the sweet - est girl talk talks of

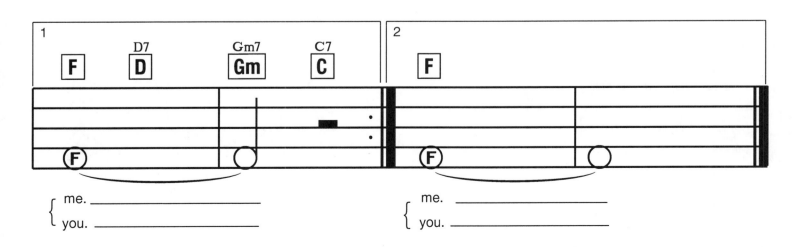

{ me. _____ / you. _____ }   { me. _____ / you. _____ }

The Glory of Love
from GUESS WHO'S COMING TO DINNER

Registration 3
Rhythm: Swing or Big Band

Words and Music by
Billy Hill

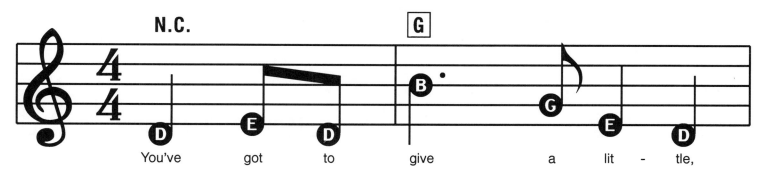

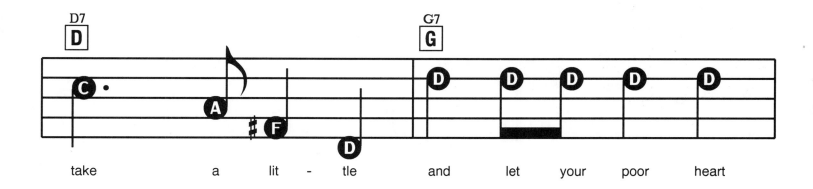

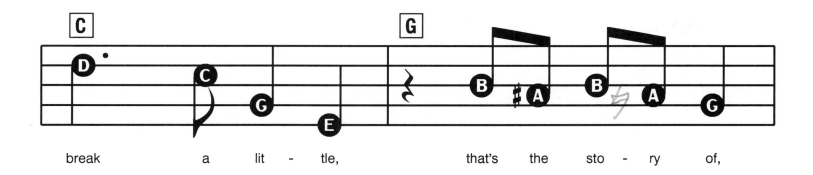

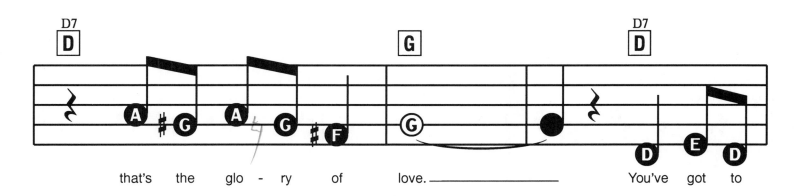

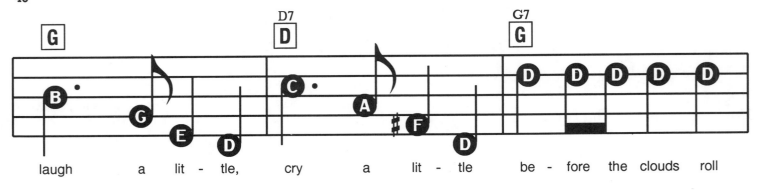

laugh a lit - tle, cry a lit - tle be - fore the clouds roll

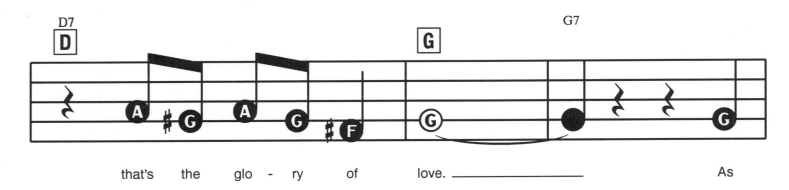

by a lit - tle, that's the sto - ry of,

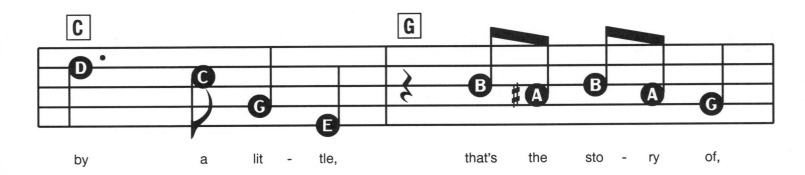

that's the glo - ry of love. _____ As

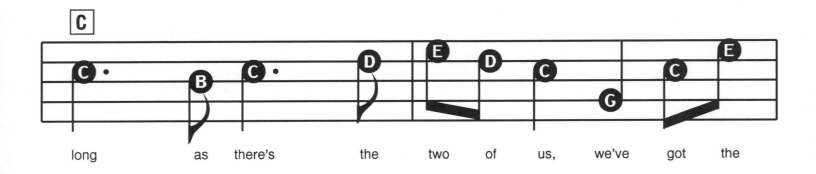

long as there's the two of us, we've got the

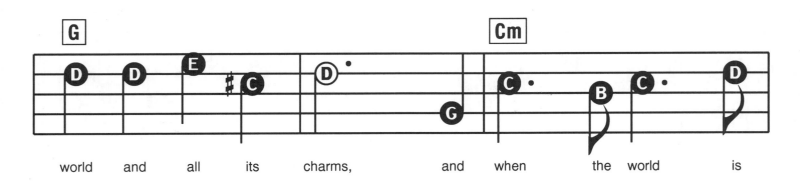

world and all its charms, and when the world is

47

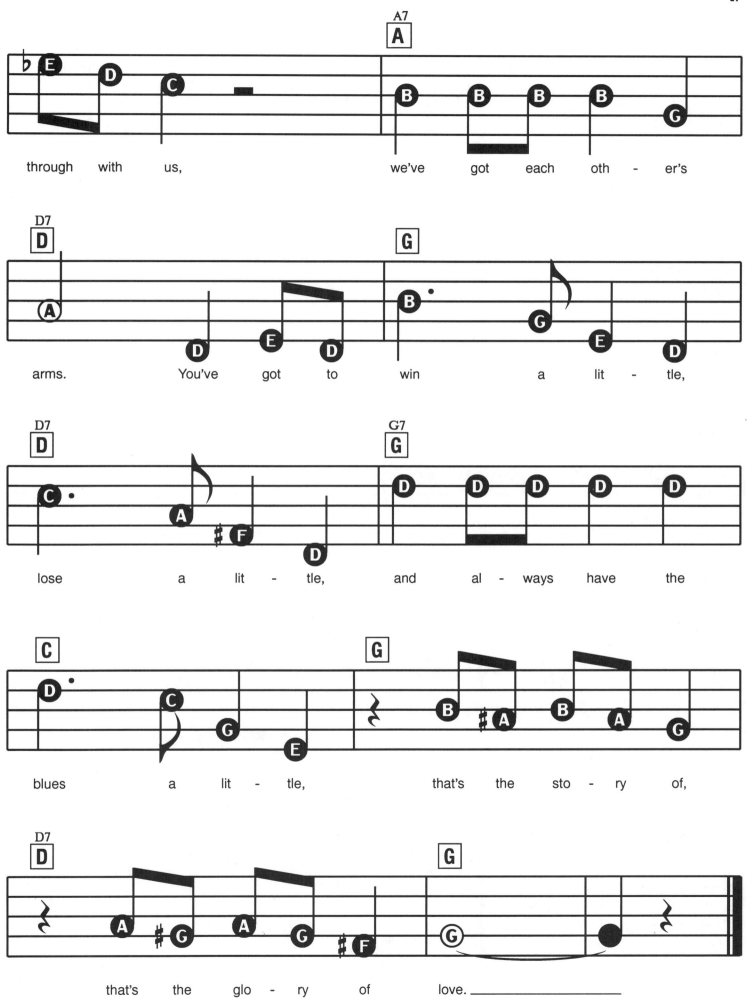

I Left My Heart in San Francisco

Registration 9
Rhythm: Fox Trot

Words by Douglas Cross
Music by George Cory

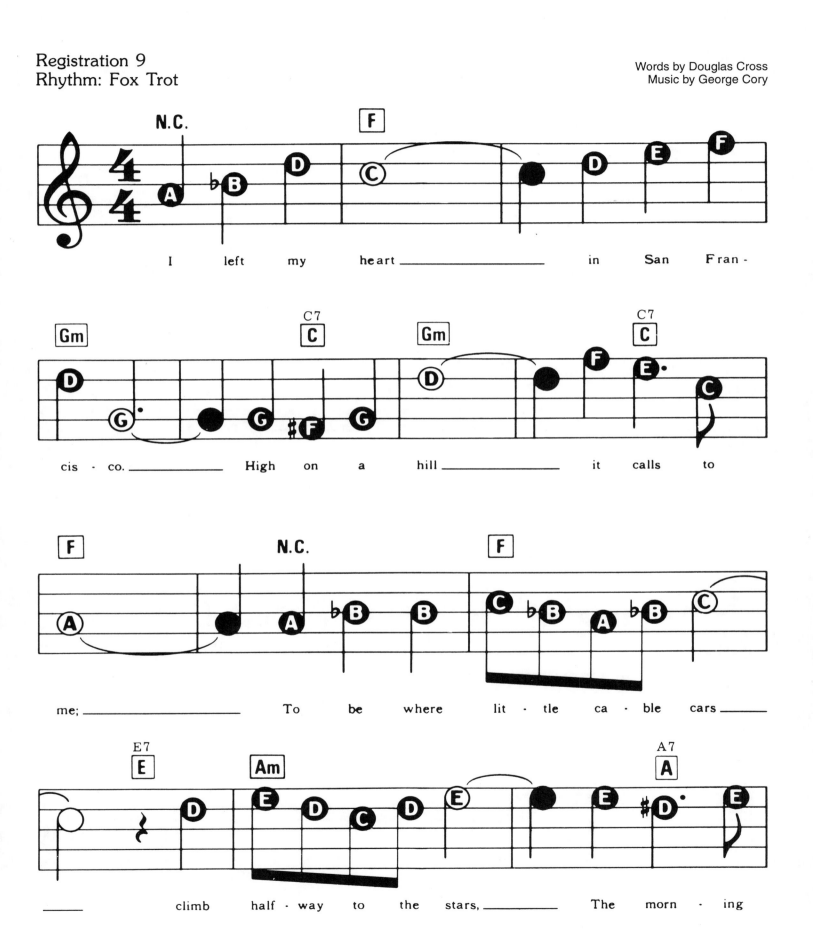

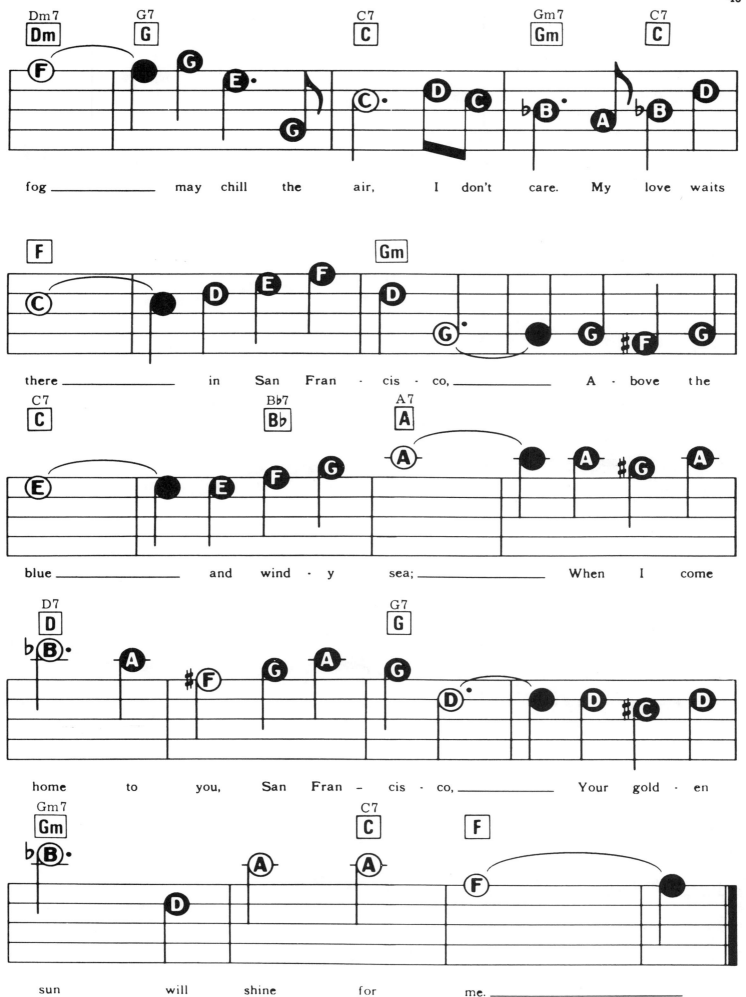

I Wish You Love

Registration 8
Rhythm: Latin

English Words by Albert Beach
French Words and Music by Charles Trenet

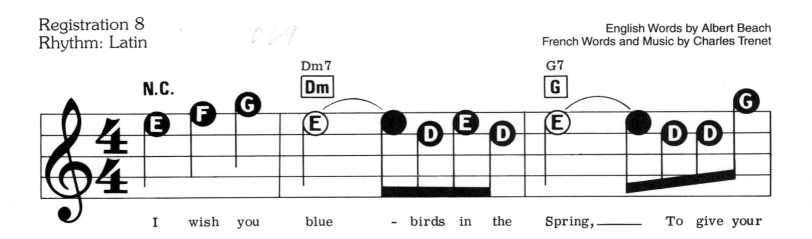

I wish you blue - birds in the Spring,_____ To give your

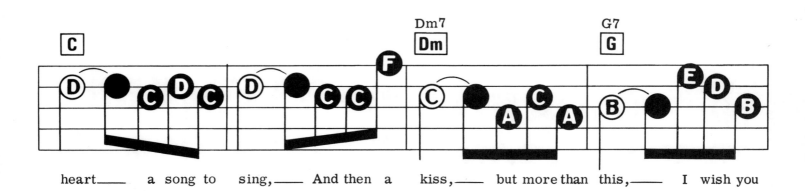

heart_____ a song to sing,_____ And then a kiss,_____ but more than this,_____ I wish you

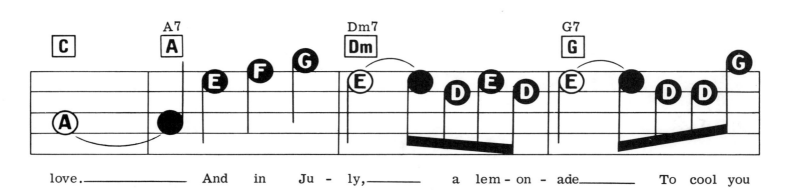

love._____ And in Ju - ly,_____ a lem - on - ade_____ To cool you

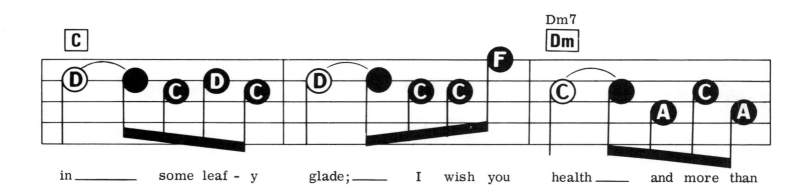

in_____ some leaf - y glade;_____ I wish you health_____ and more than

MCA music publishing

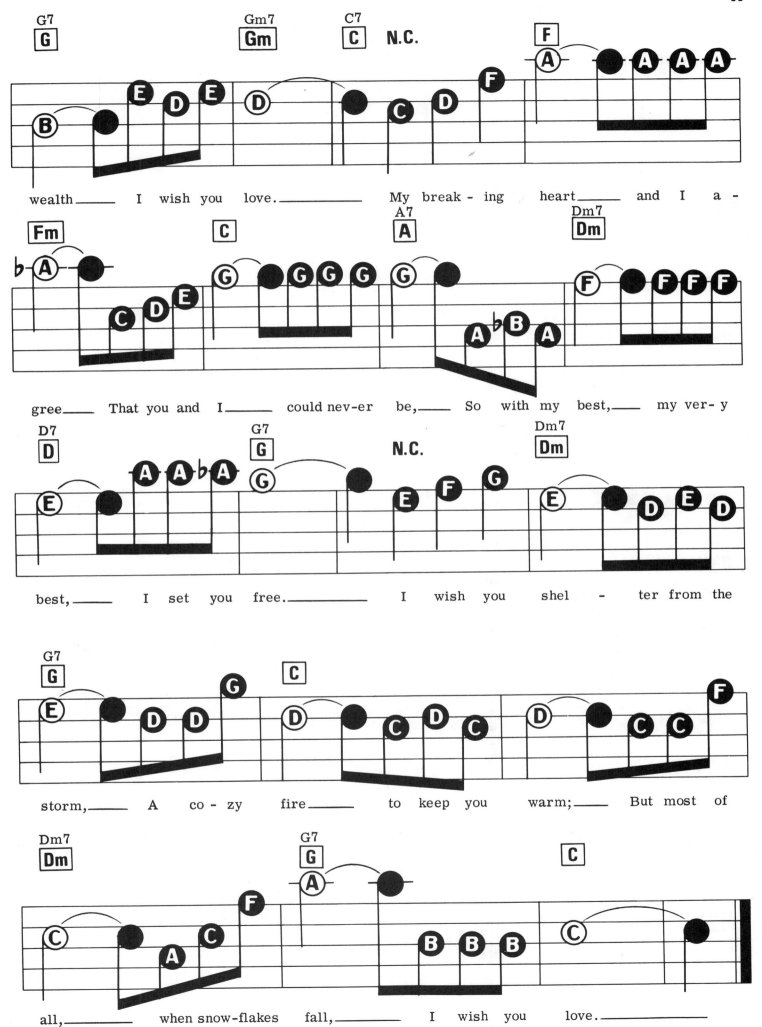

I Write the Songs

Registration 7
Rhythm: Rock or 8 Beat

Words and Music by
Bruce Johnston

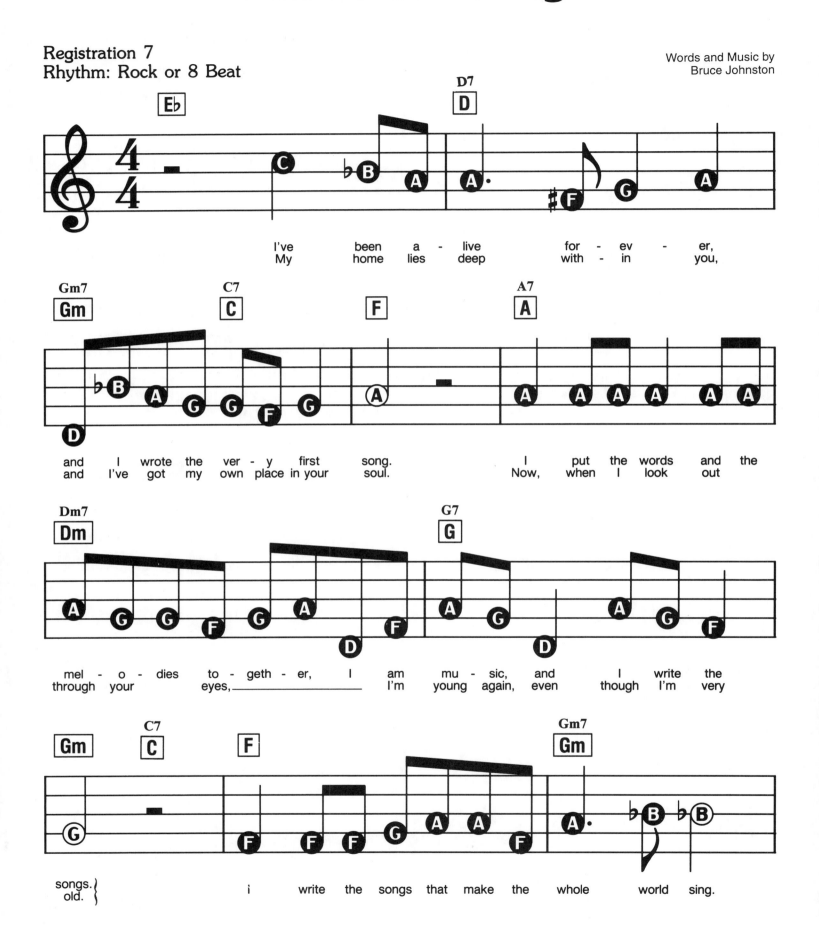

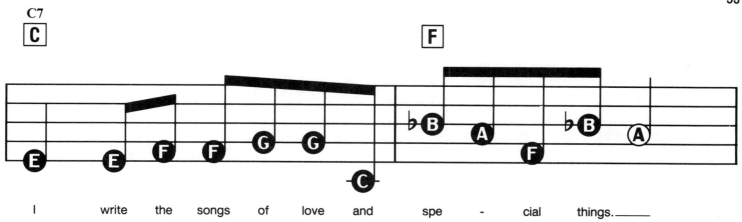

I write the songs of love and spe - cial things.____

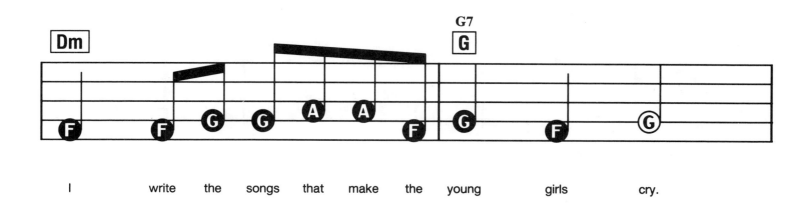

I write the songs that make the young girls cry.

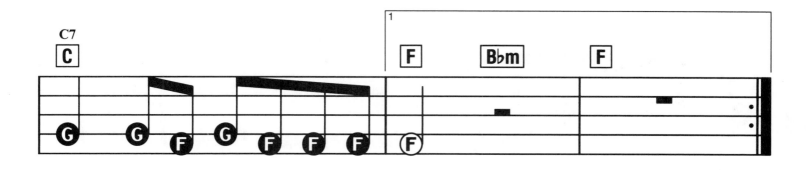

I write the songs, I write the songs.

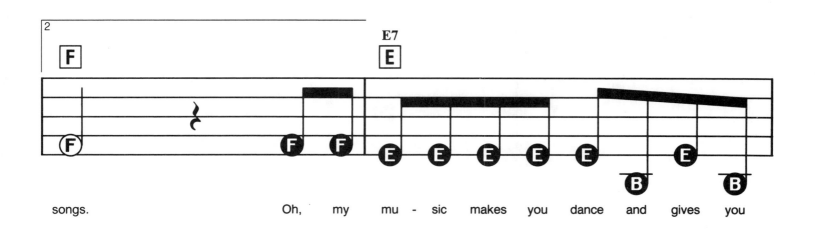

songs.   Oh, my mu - sic makes you dance and gives you

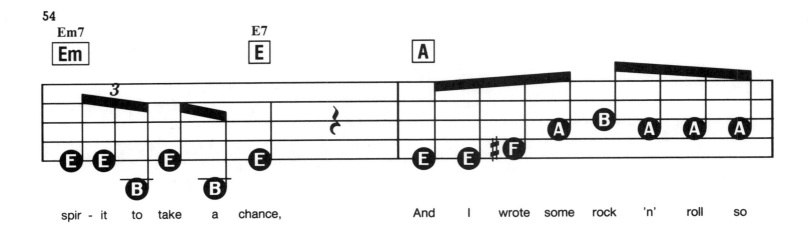

spir - it   to   take   a   chance,   And   I   wrote   some   rock   'n'   roll   so

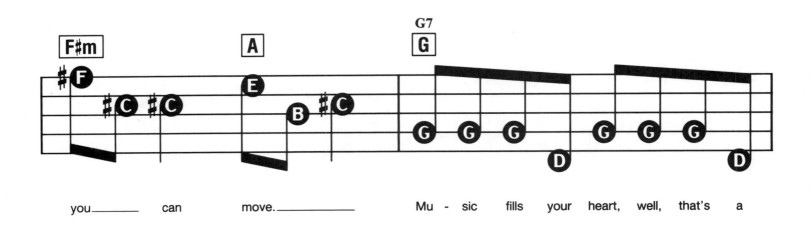

you_____   can   move._____   Mu - sic   fills   your   heart,   well,   that's   a

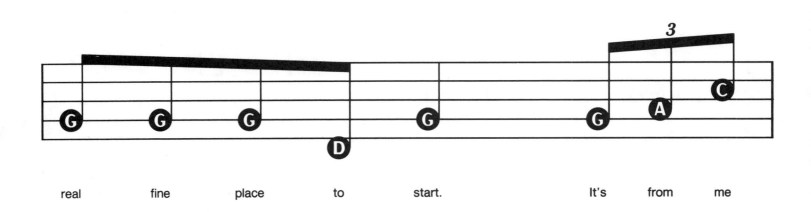

real   fine   place   to   start.   It's   from   me

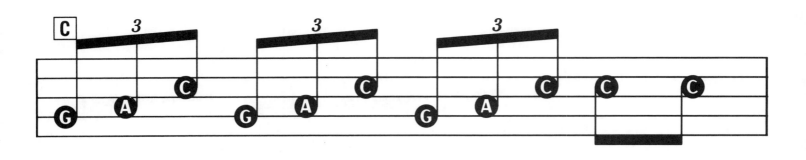

it's   for   you,   it's   from   you,   it's   for   me,   it's   a

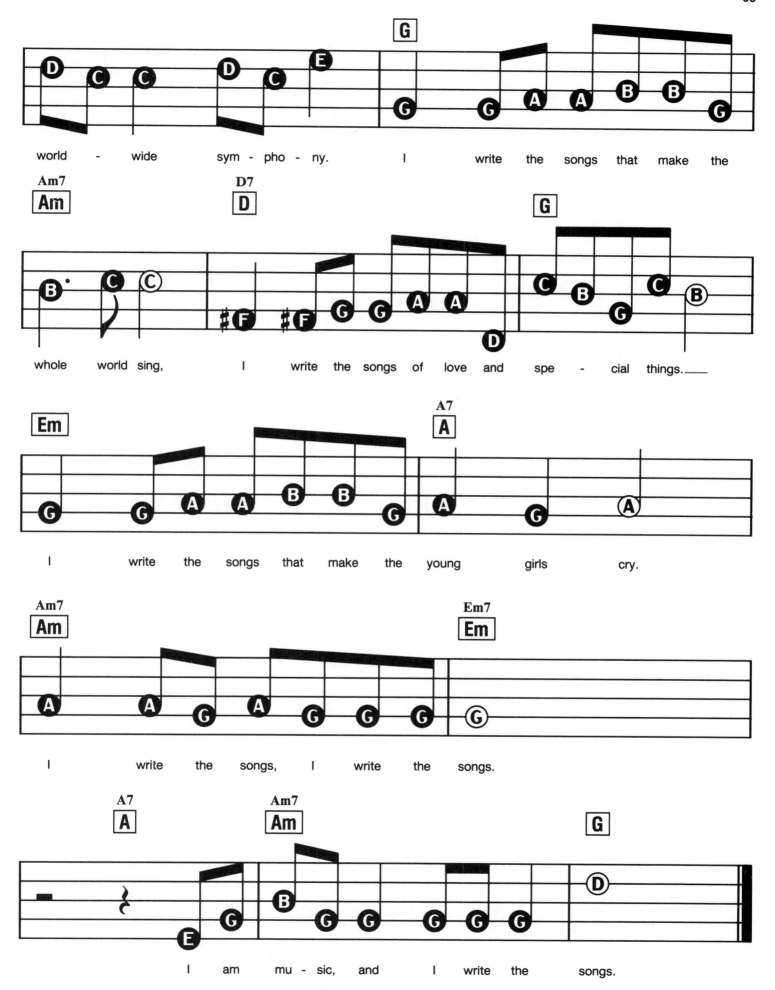

If

Registration 2
Rhythm: Slow Rock or Ballad

Words and Music by
David Gates

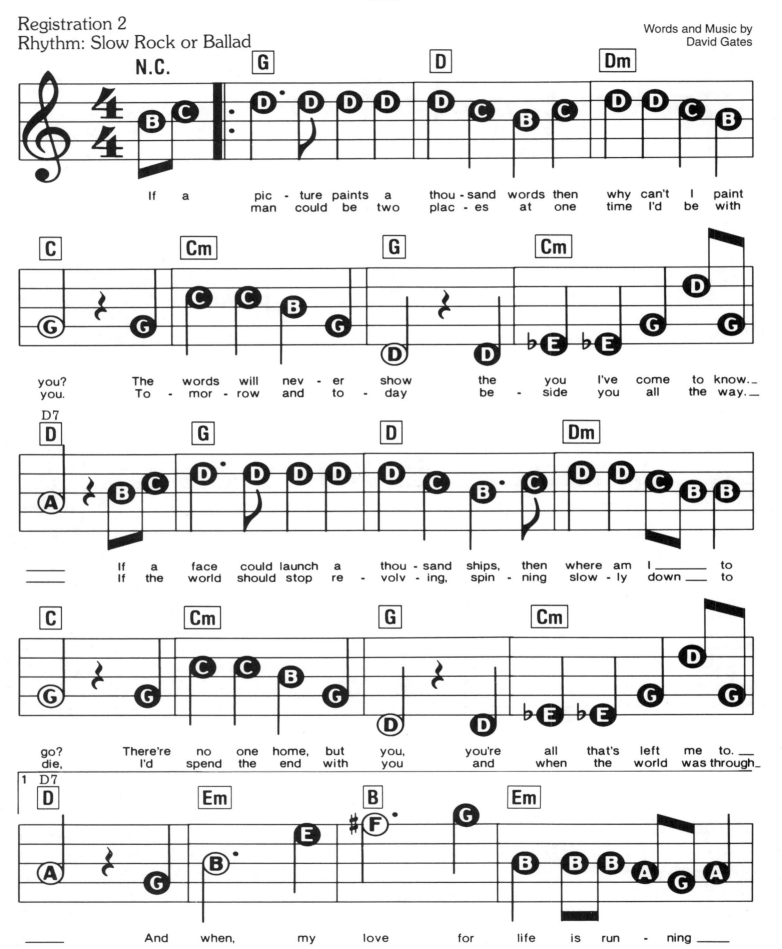

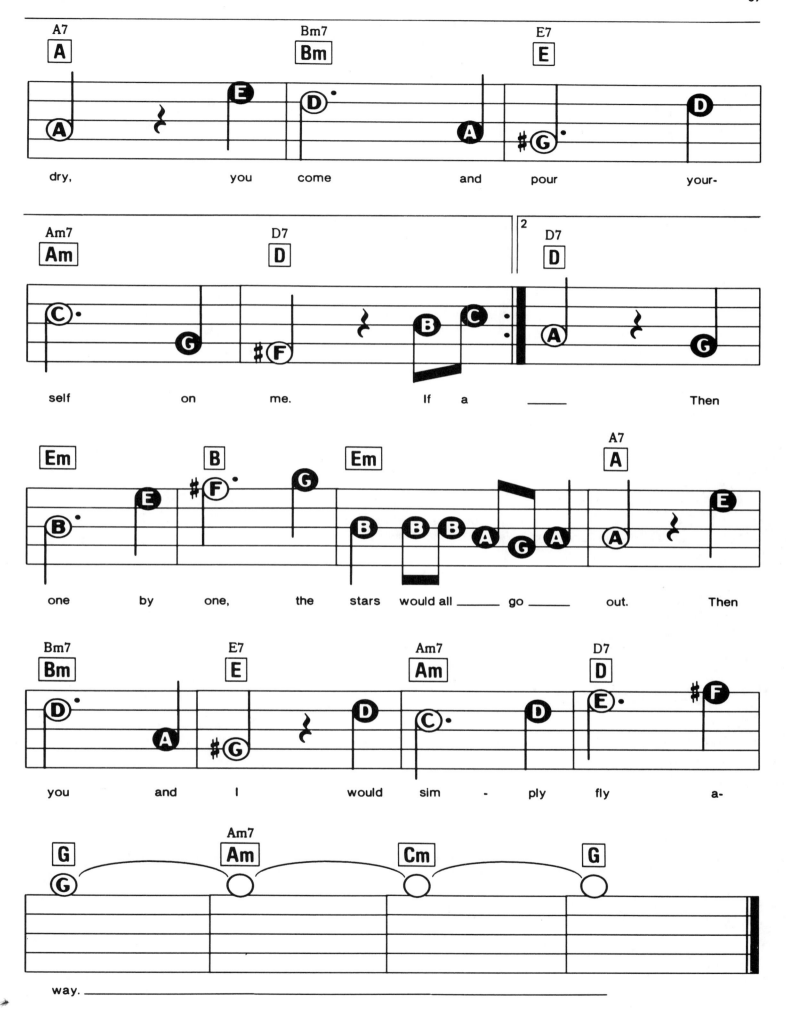

It Must Be Him
(Original French Title: "Seul Sur Son Etoile")

Words and Music by Gilbert Becaud
and Maurice Vidalin
English Adaptation by Mack David

Registration 7
Rhythm: Fox Trot or Swing

59

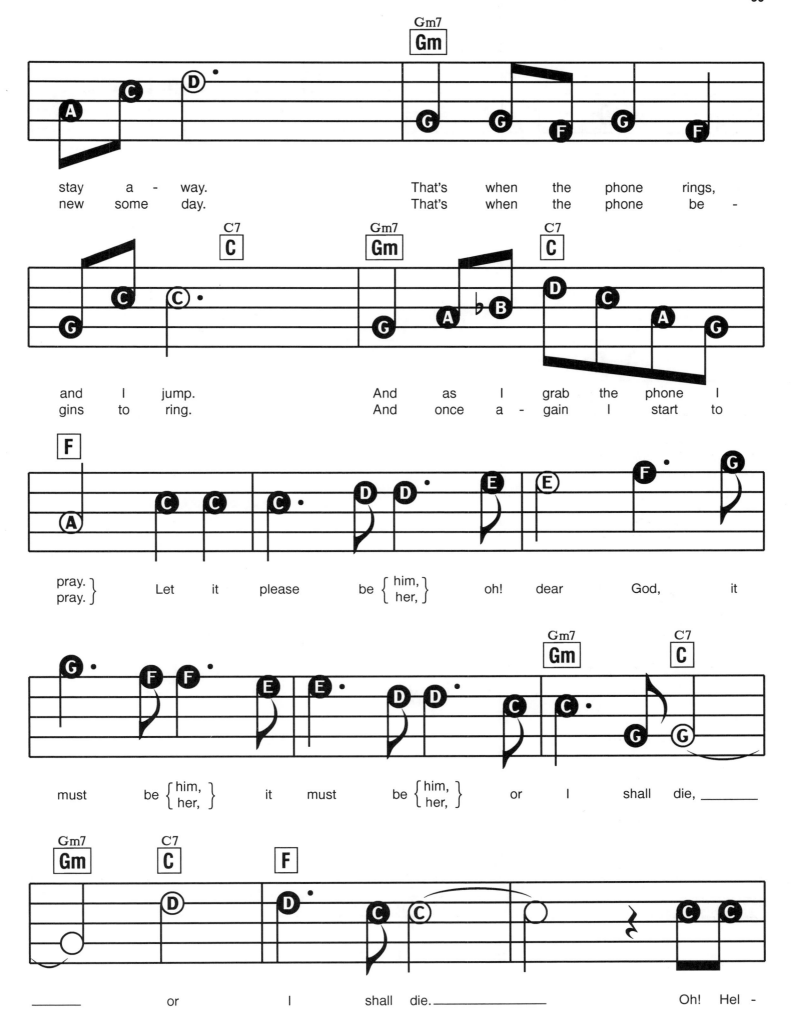

60

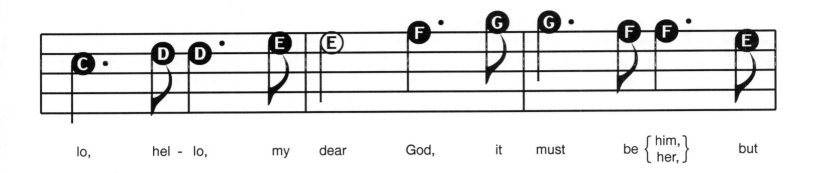

lo, hel - lo, my dear God, it must be {him, her,} but

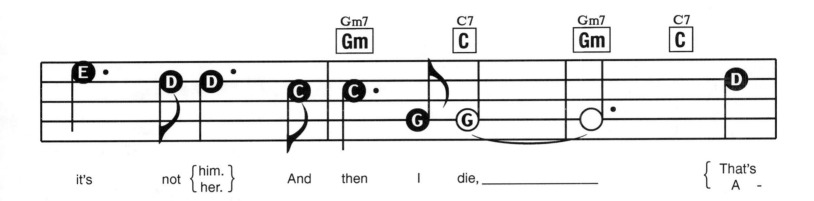

it's not {him. her.} And then I die, _____ { That's A -

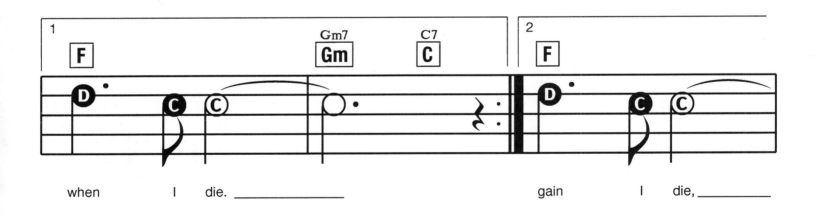

when I die. _____ gain I die, _____

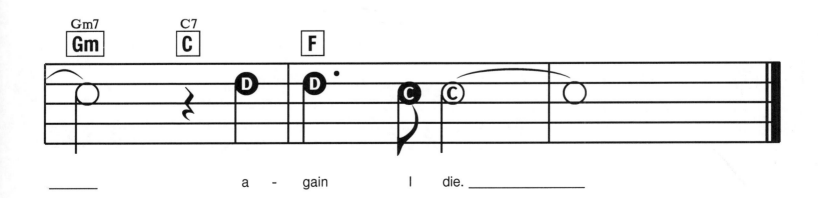

_____ a - gain I die. _____

It Was a Very Good Year

Registration 9
Rhythm: Pops or Rock

Words and Music by
Ervin Drake

62

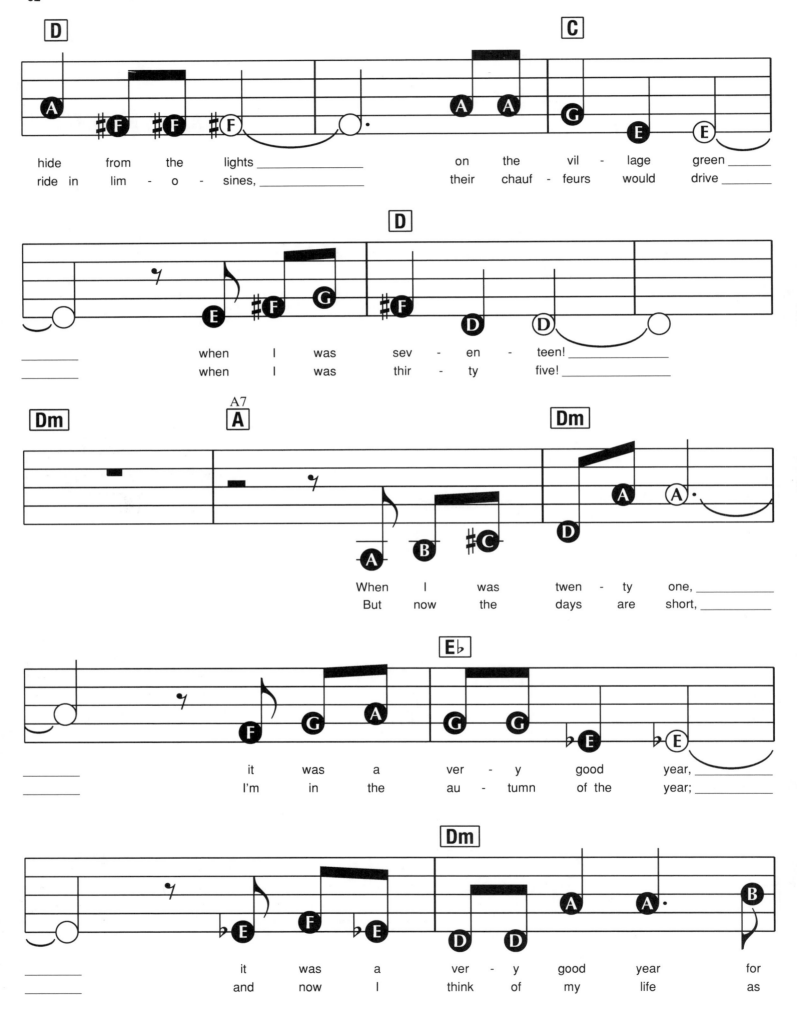

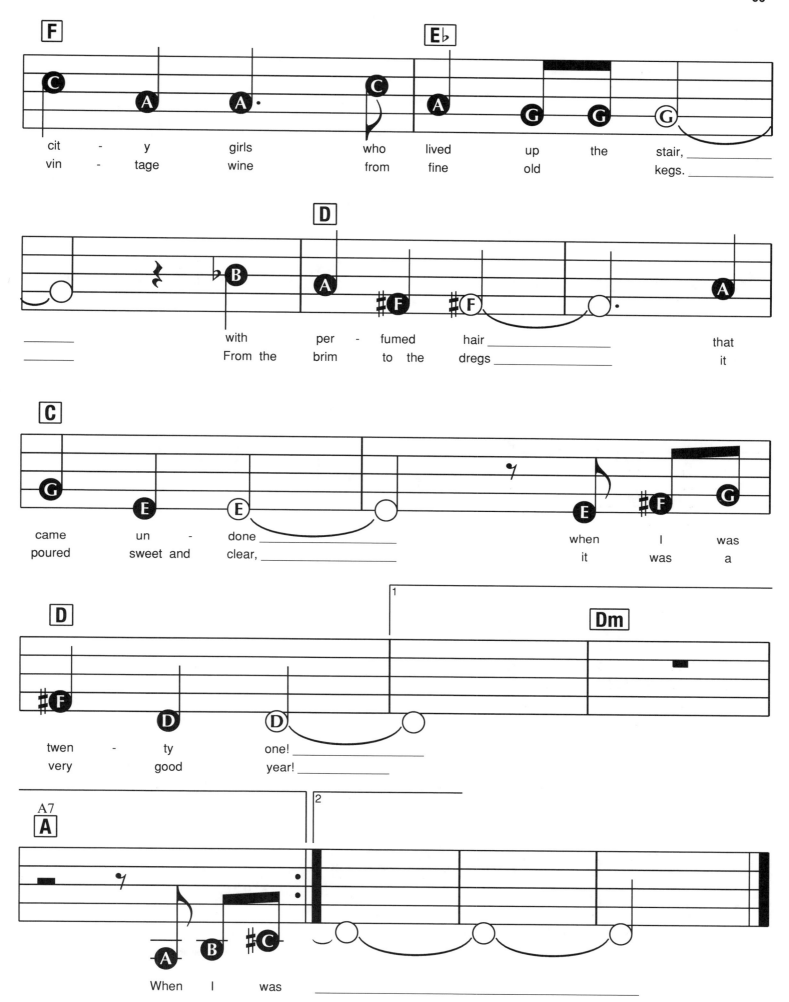

It's Not Unusual

Registration 5
Rhythm: Rock

Words and Music by Gordon Mills
and Les Reed

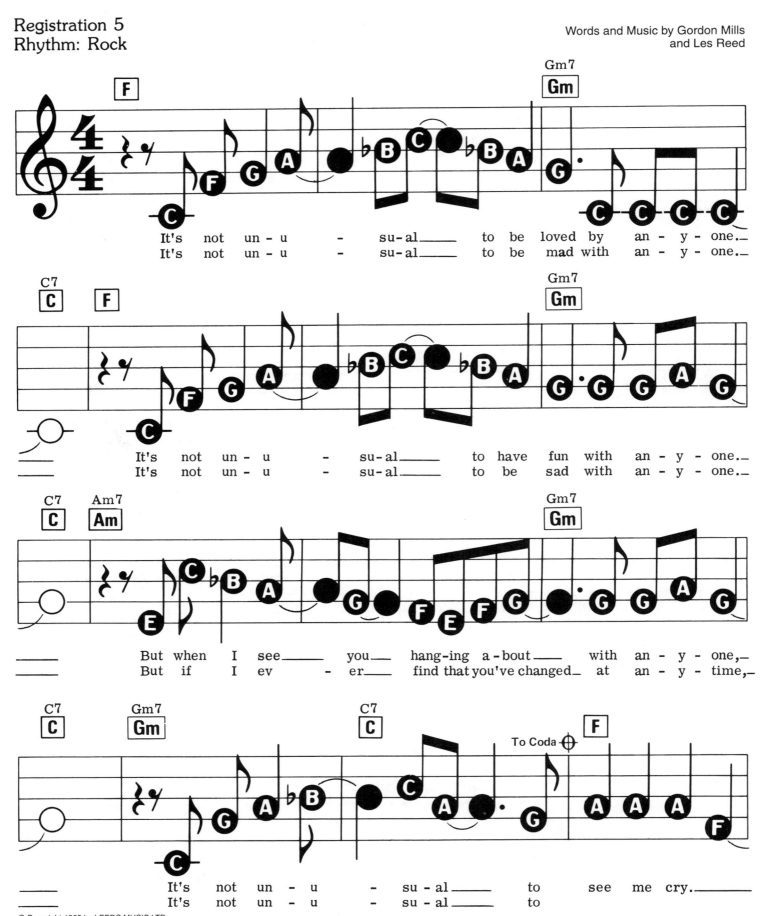

MCA music publishing

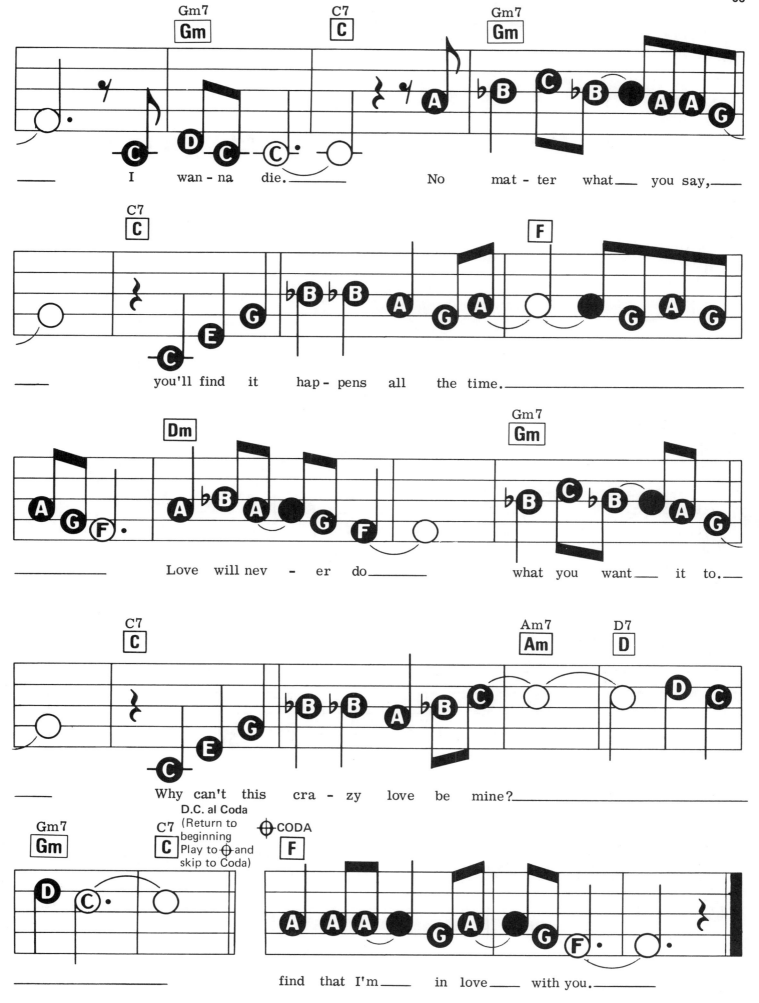

Lollipops and Roses

Registration 2
Rhythm: Waltz or Jazz Waltz

Words and Music by
Tony Velona

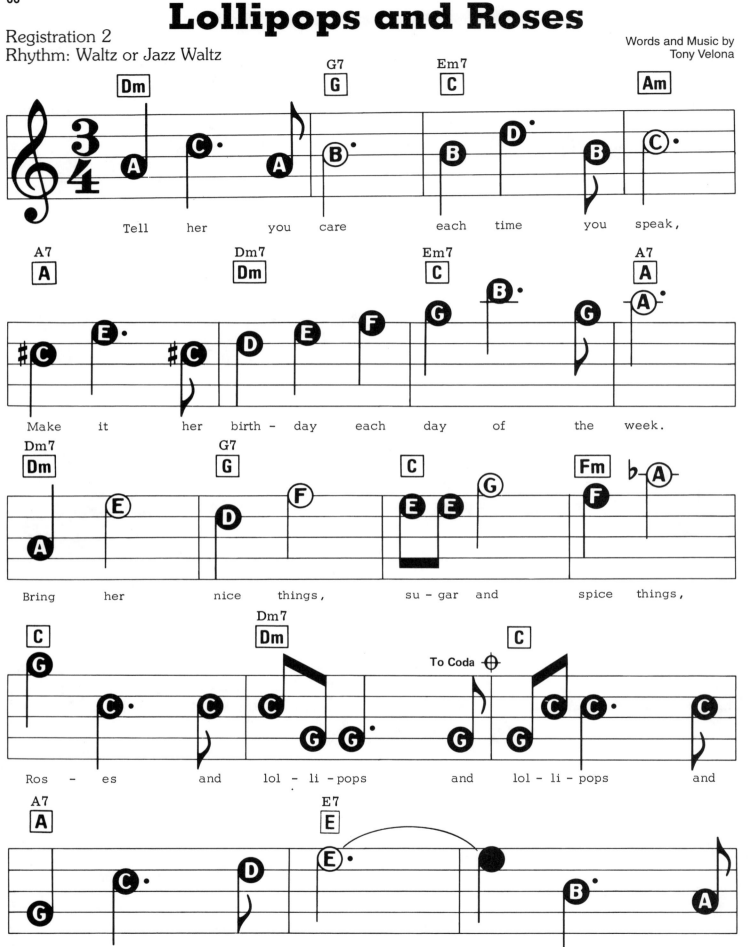

MCA music publishing

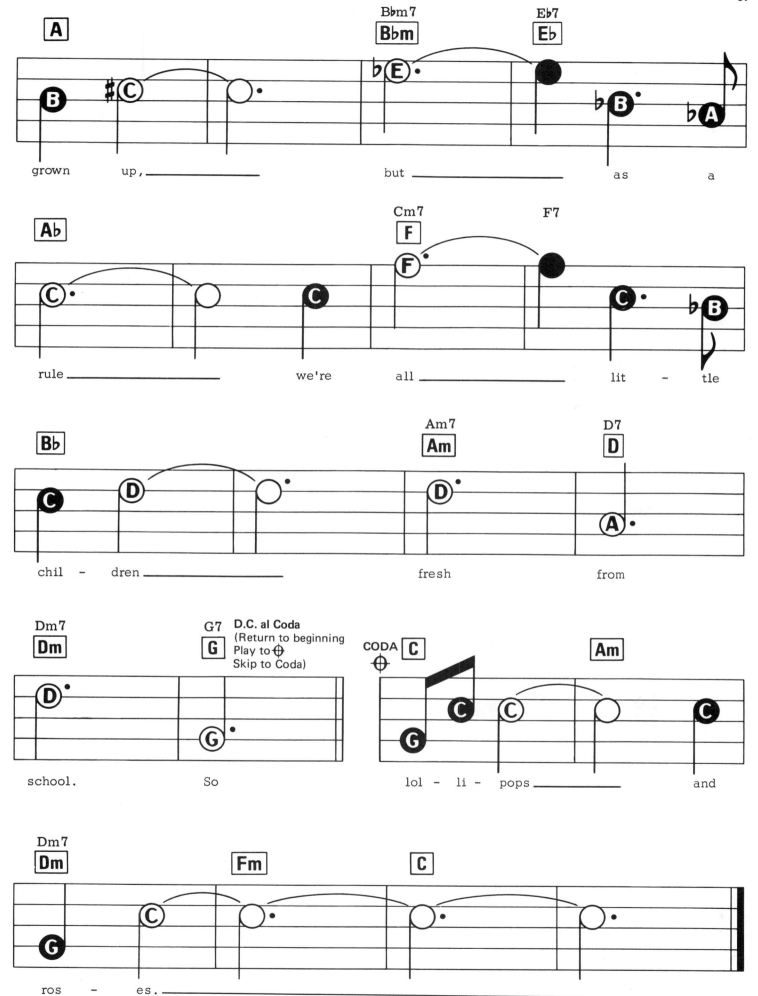

The Look of Love
from CASINO ROYALE

Registration 4
Rhythm: Bossa Nova

Words by Hal David
Music by Burt Bacharach

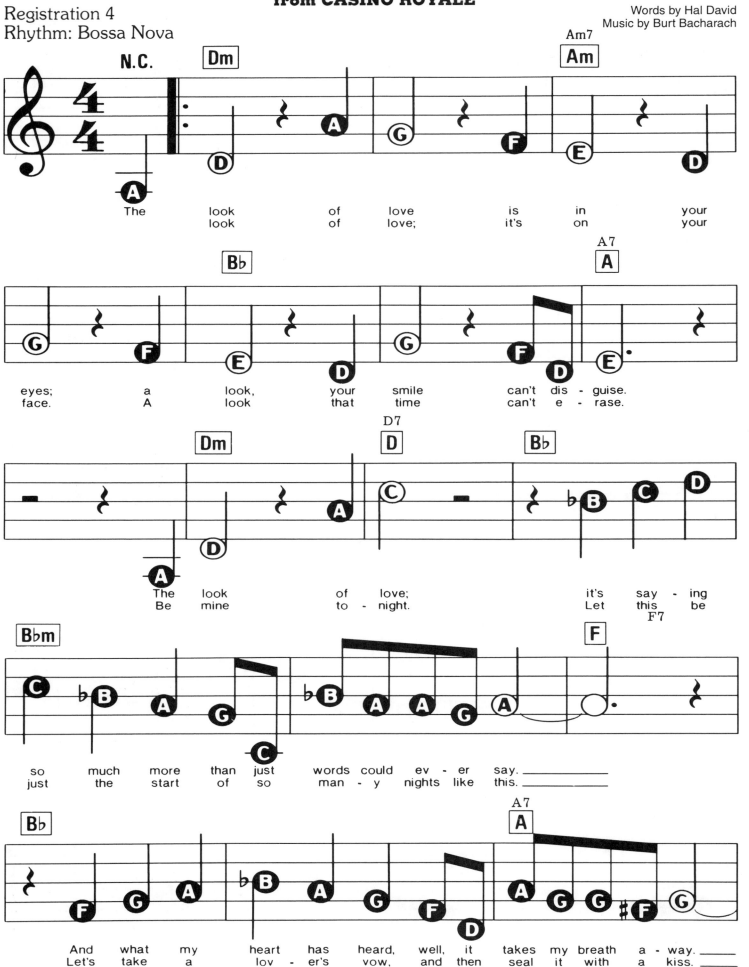

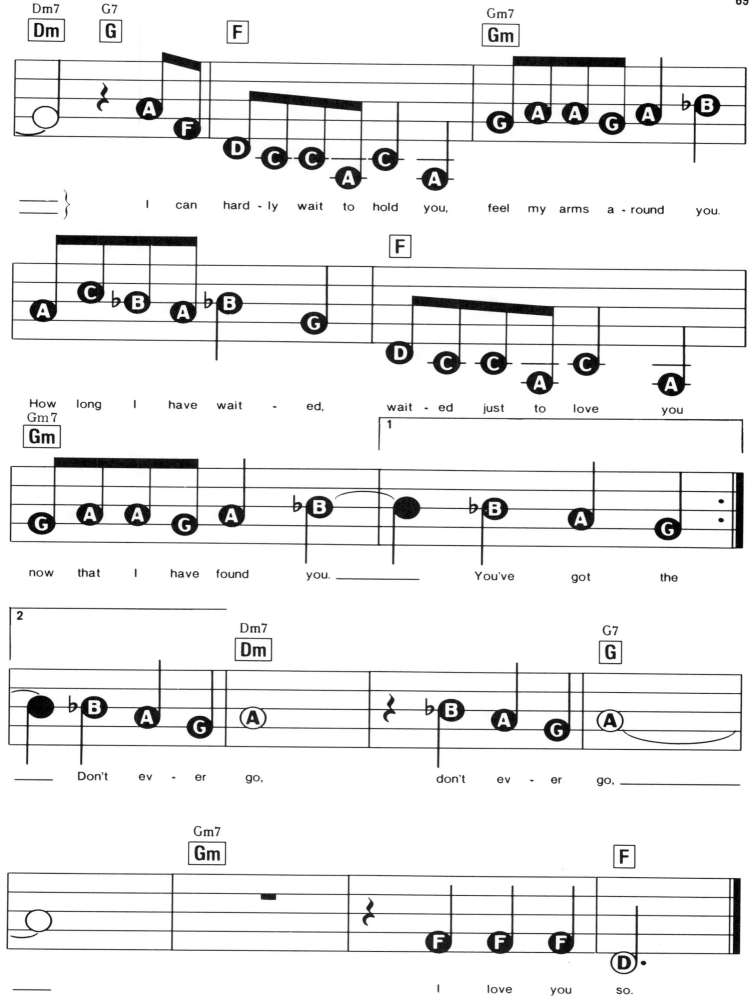

L-O-V-E

Registration 8
Rhythm: Fox Trot or Swing

Words and Music by Bert Kaempfert
and Milt Gabler

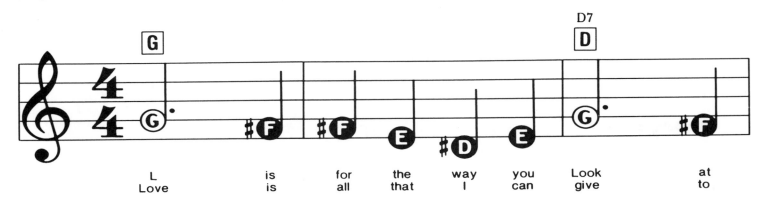

L   is   for   the   way   you   Look   at
Love   is   for all   that   I   can   give   to

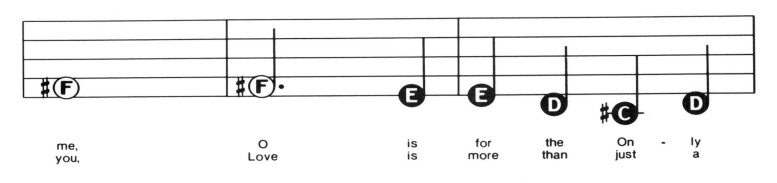

me,   O   is   for   the   On   -   ly
you,   Love   is   for more   than   just   a

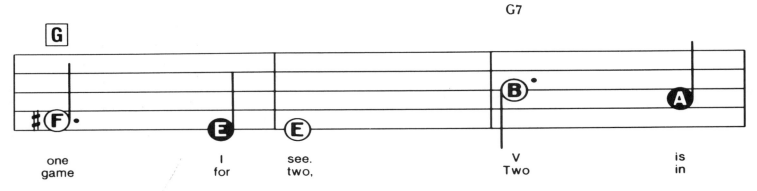

one   I   see.   V   is
game   for   two,   Two   in

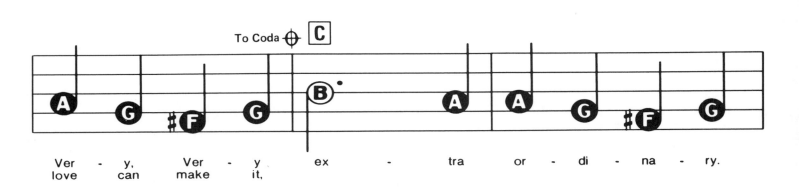

Ver - y,   Ver   - y   ex   -   tra   or - di - na - ry.
love   can make   it,

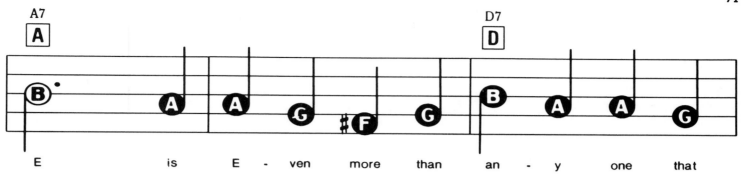

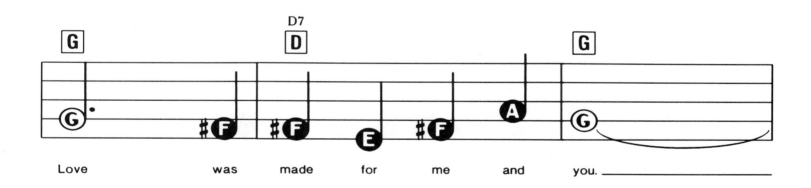

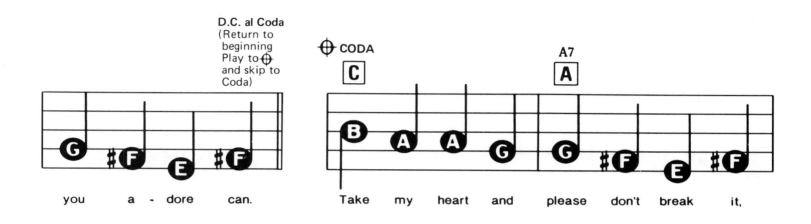

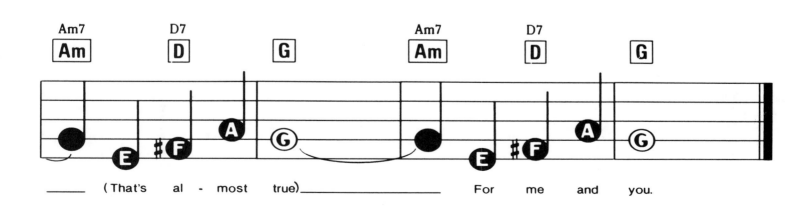

A Man and a Woman
(Un Homme Et Une Femme)
from A MAN AND A WOMAN

Original Words by Pierre Barouh
English Words by Jerry Keller
Music by Francis Lai

Registration 5
Rhythm: Fox Trot

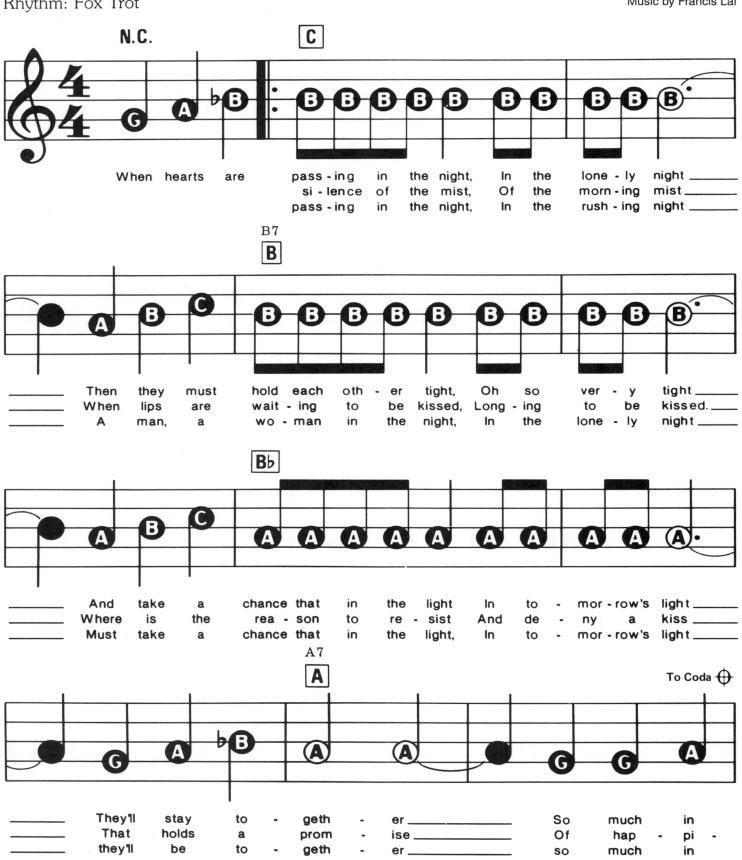

MCA music publishing

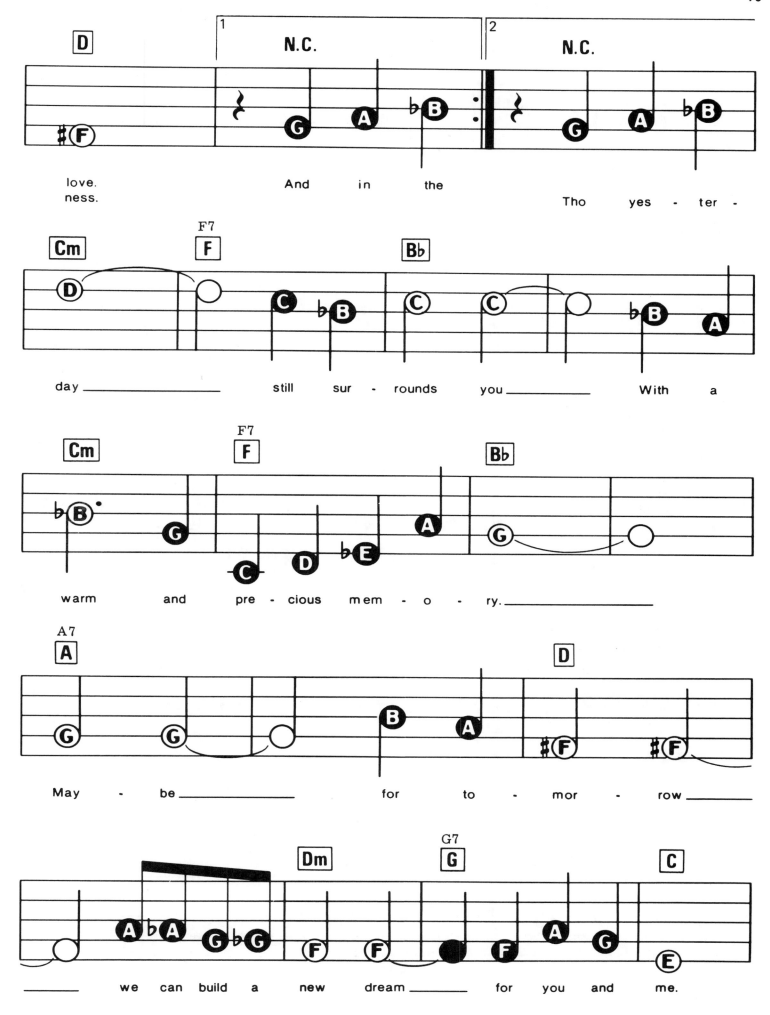

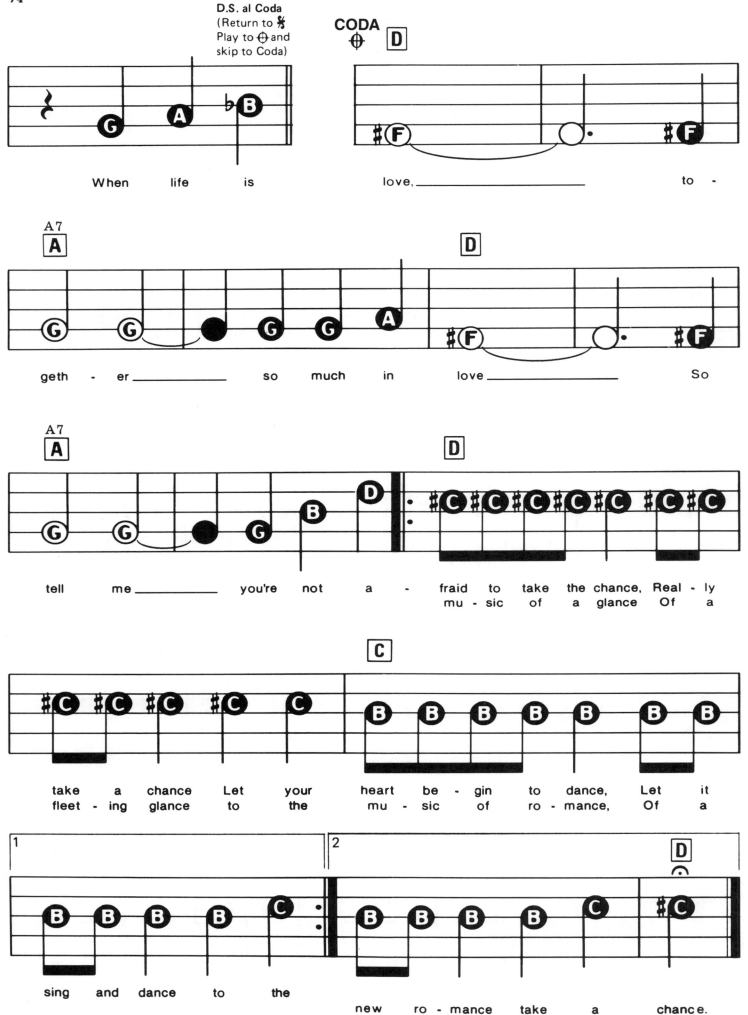

Wives and Lovers
(Hey, Little Girl)
from the Paramount Picture WIVES AND LOVERS

Registration 1
Rhythm: Waltz or Jazz Waltz

Words by Hal David
Music by Burt Bacharach

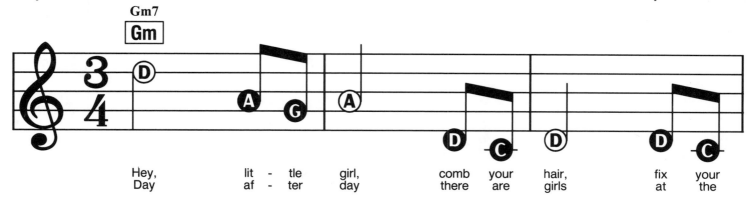

Hey,   lit - tle girl,   comb   your hair,   fix   your
Day   af - ter day   there   are girls   at   the

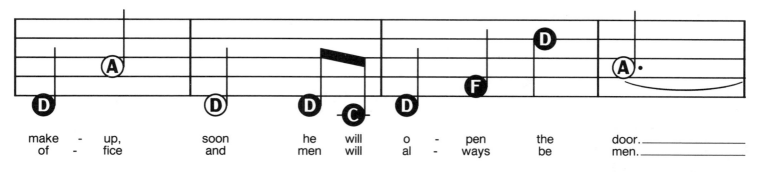

make - up,   soon   he   will o - pen the   door.
of - fice   and   men   will al - ways be   men.

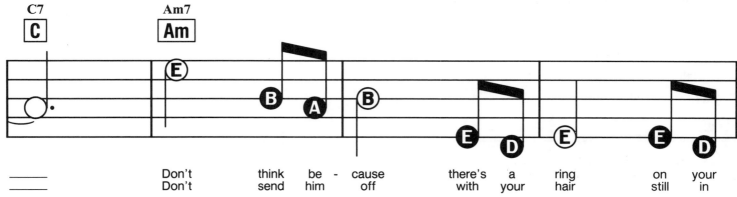

_____   Don't   think be - cause   there's a   ring   on   your
_____   Don't   send   him off   with   your   hair   still   in

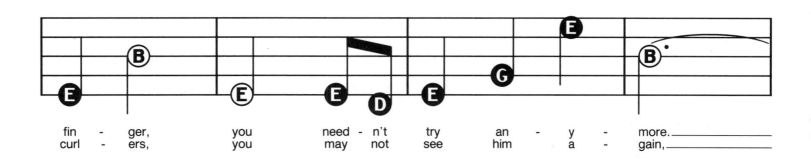

fin - ger,   you   need - n't try   an - y - more.
curl - ers,   you   may   not see   him   a - gain,

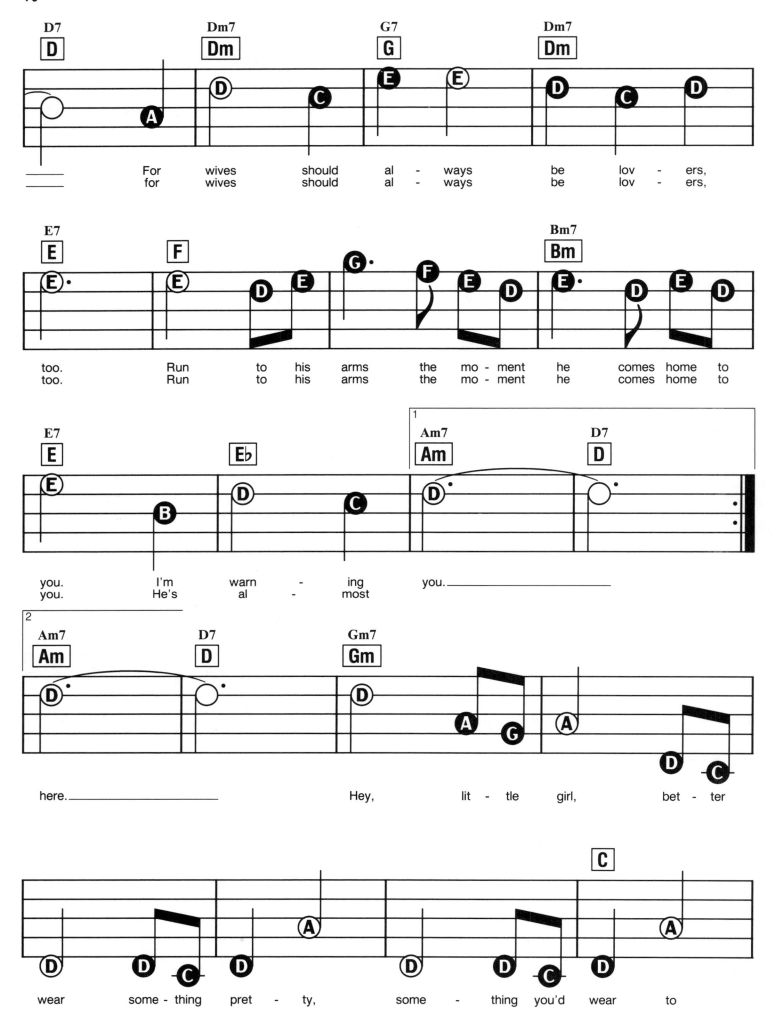

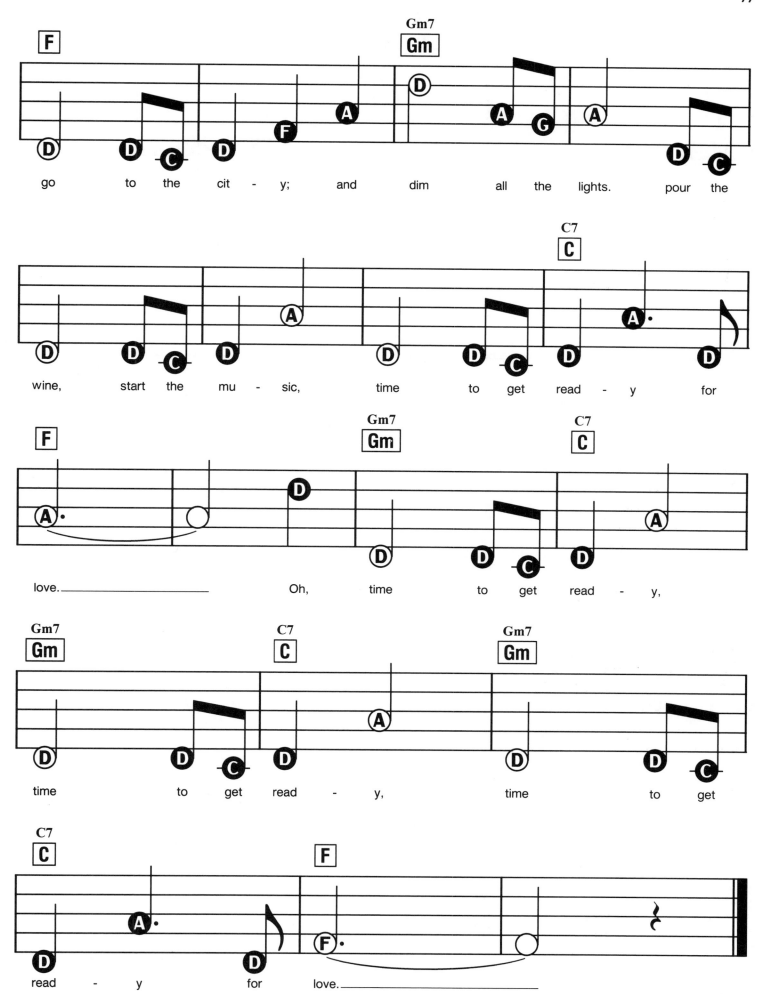

Meditation
(Meditacáo)

English Words by Norman Gimbel
Original Words by Newton Mendonca
Music by Antonio Carlos Jobim

Registation 5
Rhythm: Rhumba or Latin

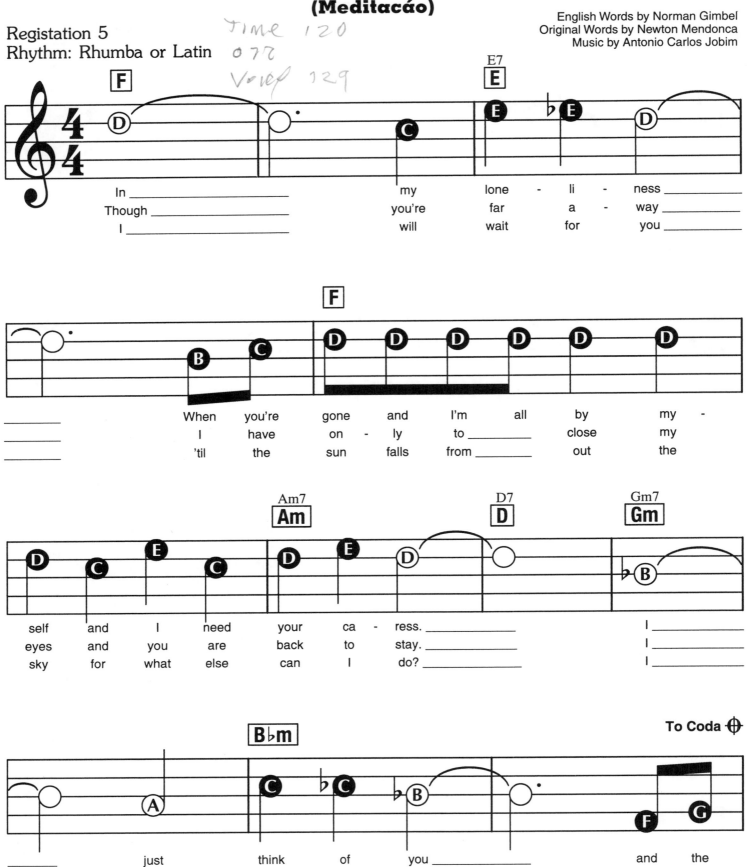

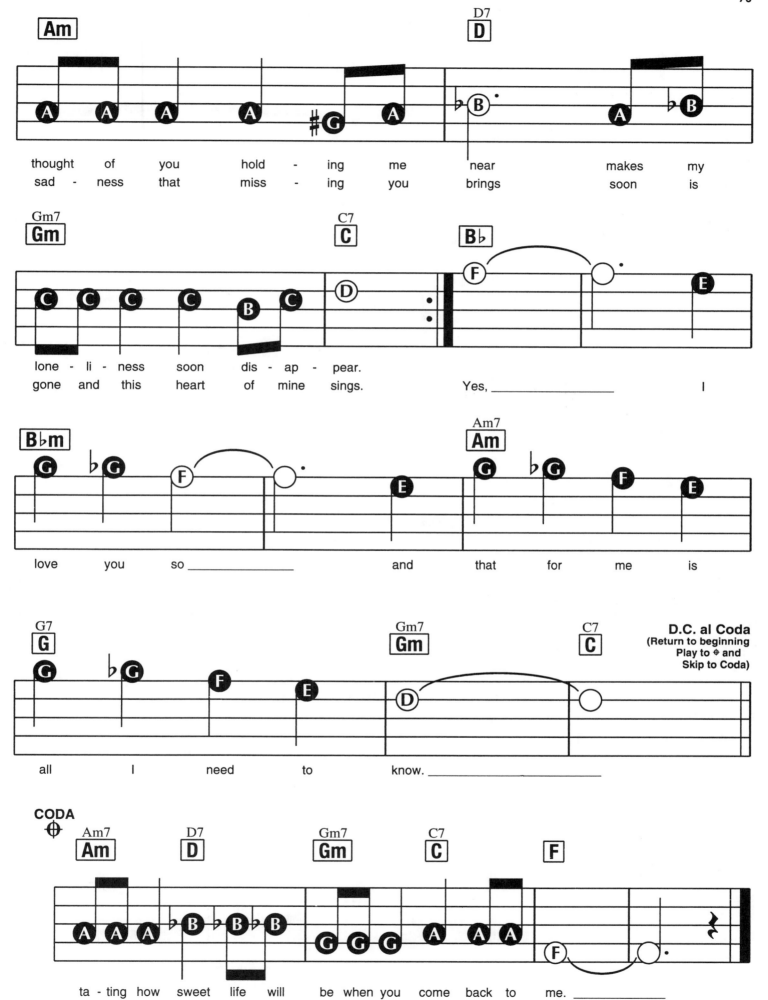

Misty

Registration 8
Rhythm: Swing or Jazz

Words by Johnny Burke
Music by Erroll Garner

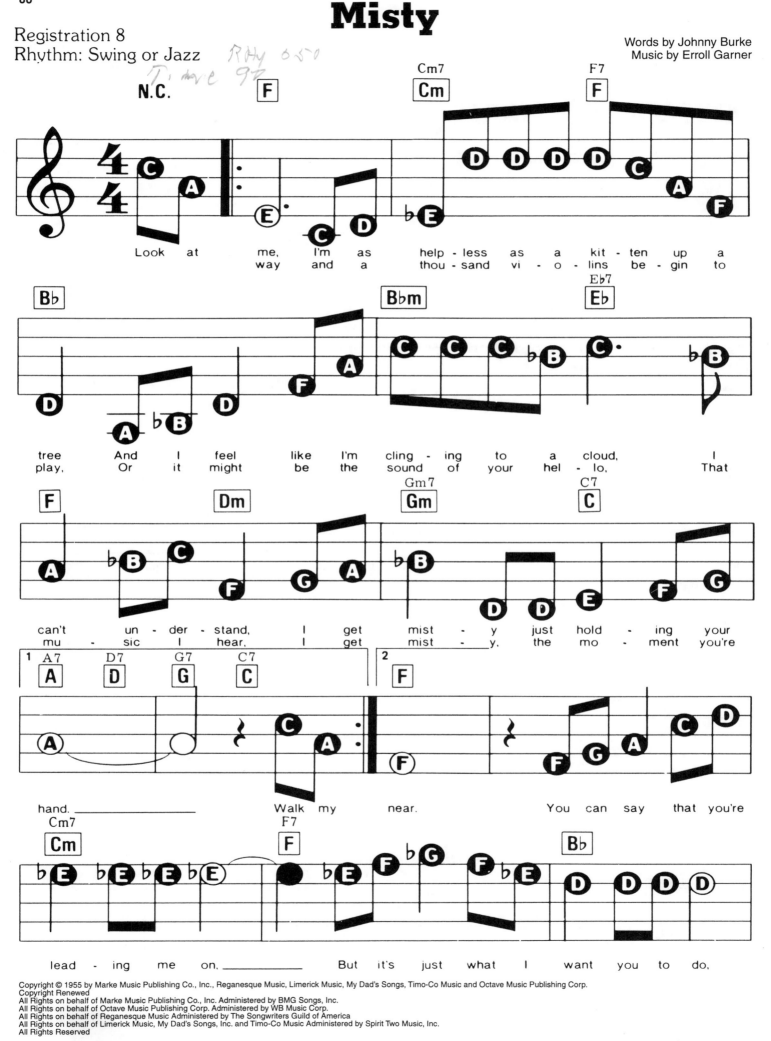

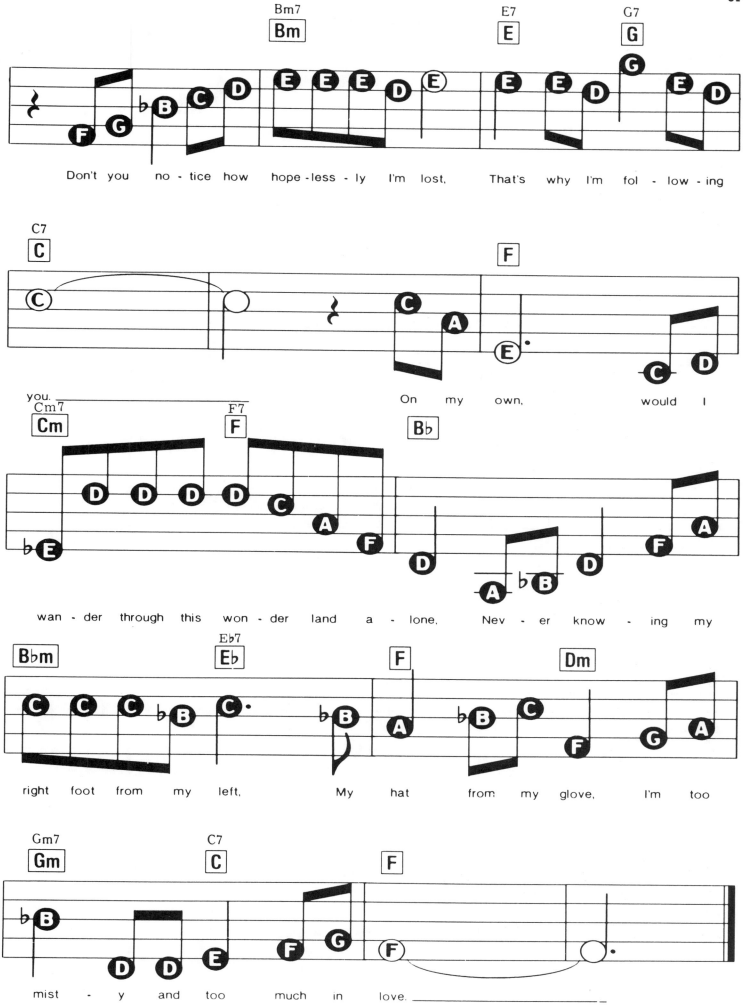

Mona Lisa
from the Paramount Picture CAPTAIN CAREY, U.S.A.

Registration 9
Rhythm: Swing or 8 Beat

Words and Music by Jay Livingston
and Ray Evans

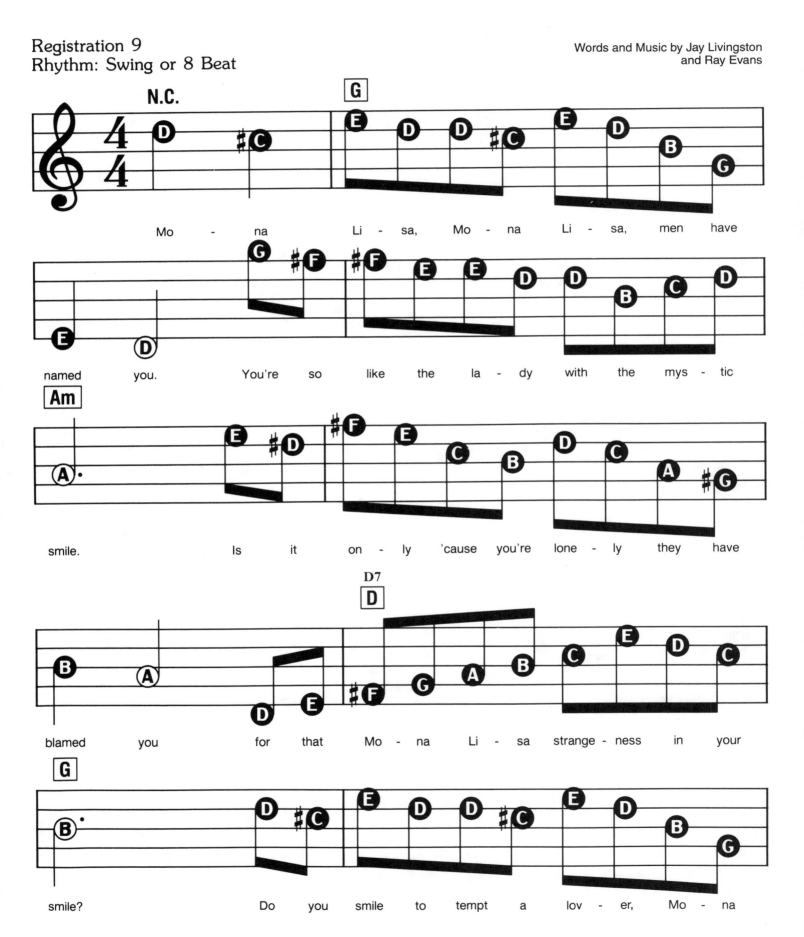

83

Moon River
from the Paramount Picture BREAKFAST AT TIFFANY'S

Registration 3
Rhythm: Waltz

Words by Johnny Mercer
Music by Henry Mancini

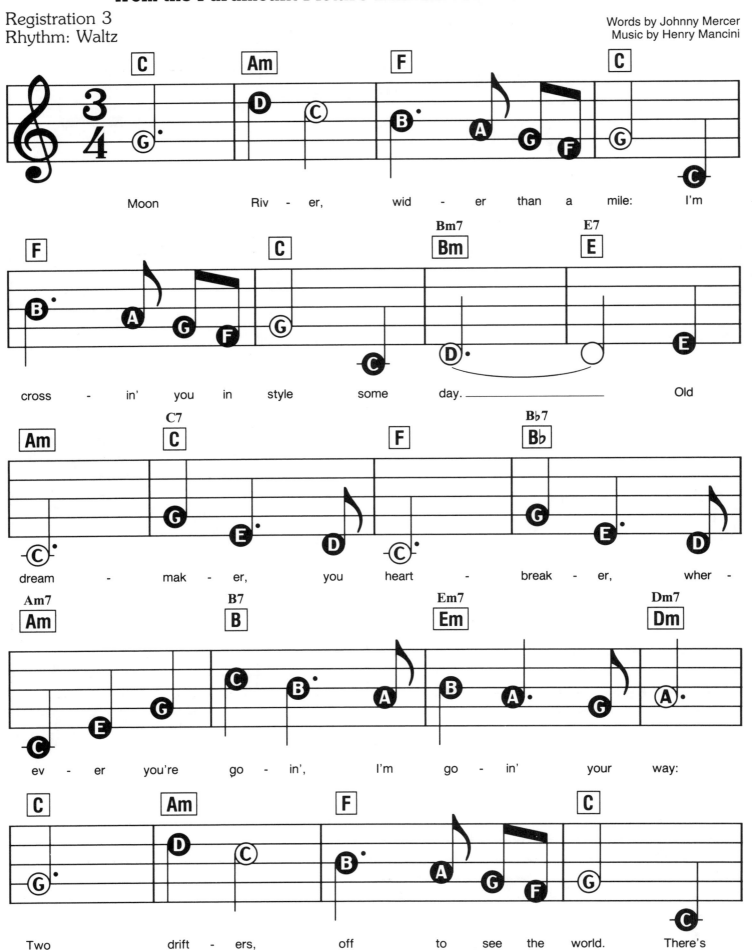

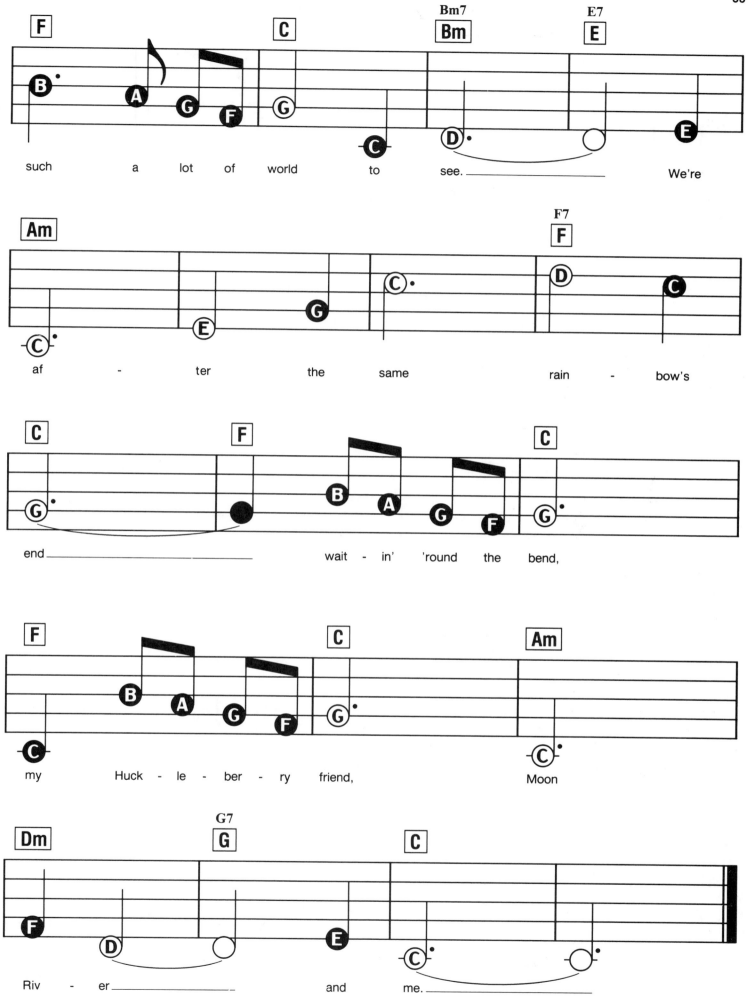

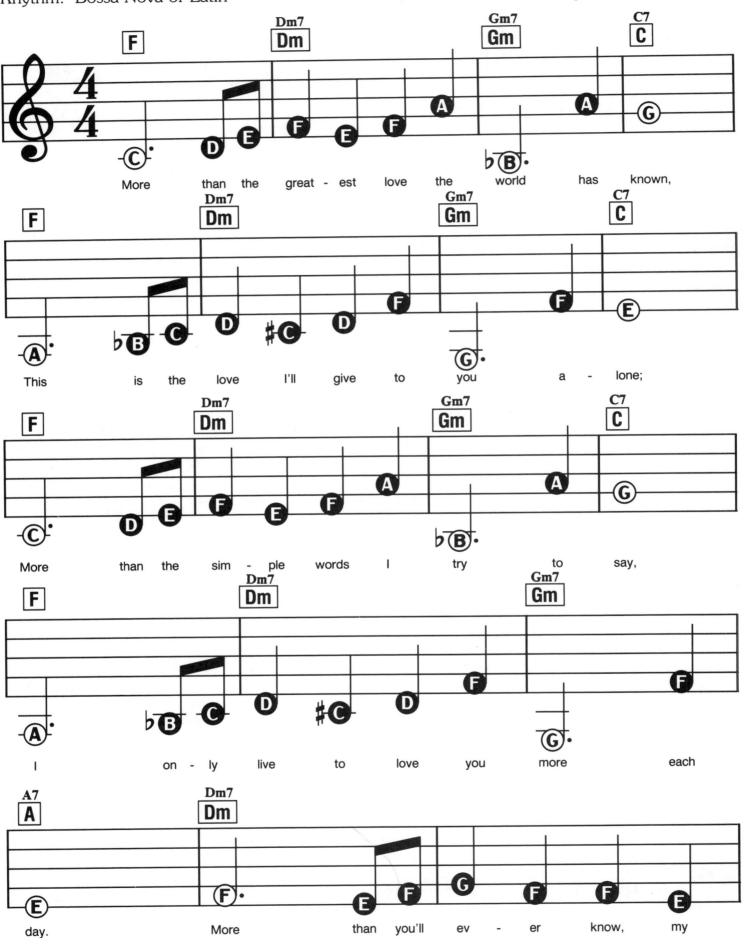

More
(Ti Guardero' Nel Cuore)
from the film MONDO CANE

Registration 2
Rhythm: Bossa Nova or Latin

Music by Nino Oliviero and Riz Ortolani
Italian Lyrics by Marcello Ciorciolini
English Lyrics by Norman Newell

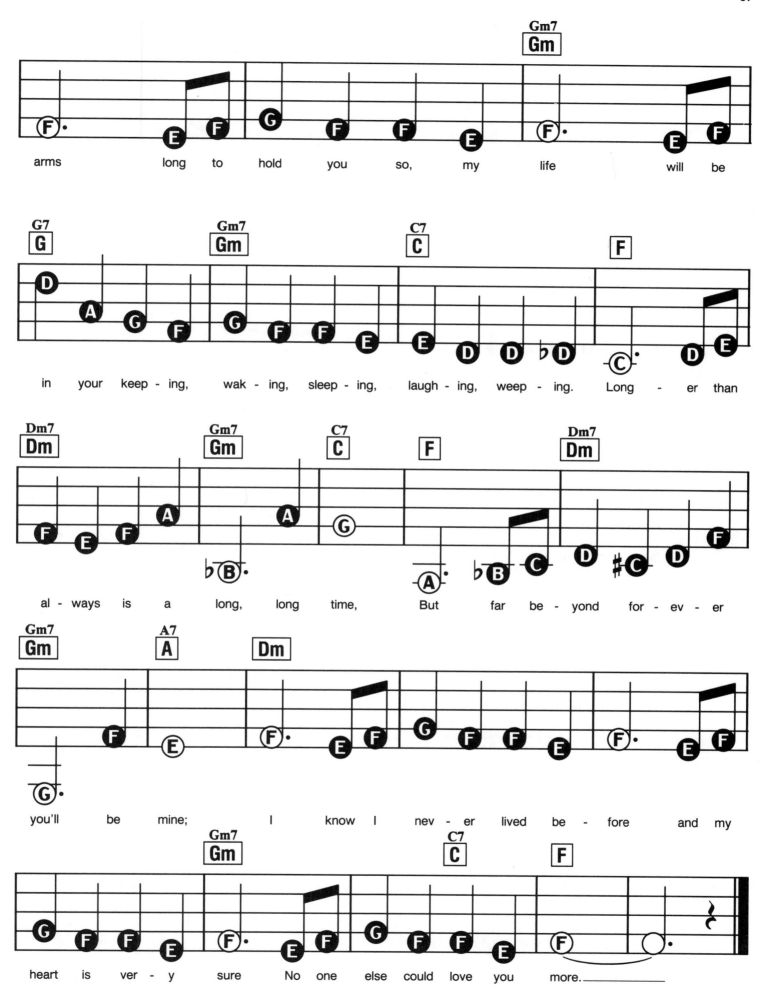

Satin Doll
from SOPHISTICATED LADIES

Registration 4
Rhythm: Swing or Jazz

Words by Johnny Mercer and Billy Strayhorn
Music by Duke Ellington

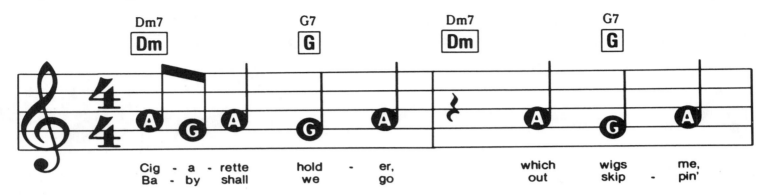

Cig - a - rette hold - er, which wigs me,
Ba - by shall we go out skip - pin'

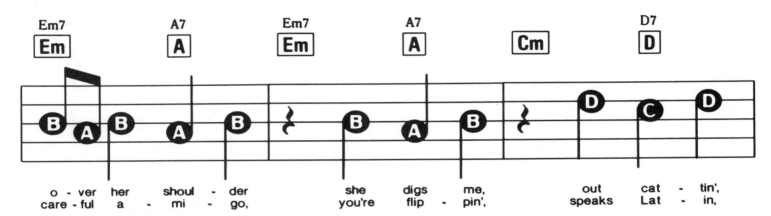

o - ver her shoul - der she digs me, out cat - tin',
care - ful a - mi - go, you're flip - pin', out speaks Lat - in,

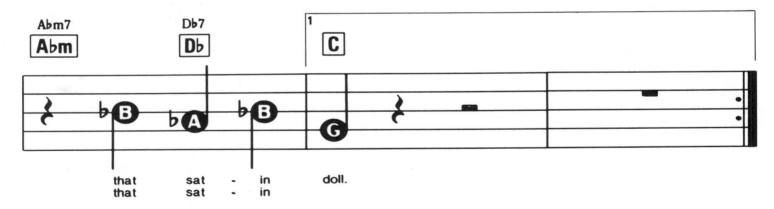

that sat - in doll.
that sat - in

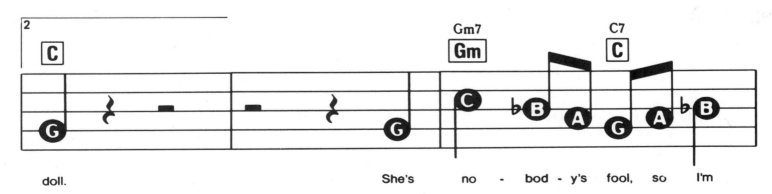

doll.

She's no - bod - y's fool, so I'm

89

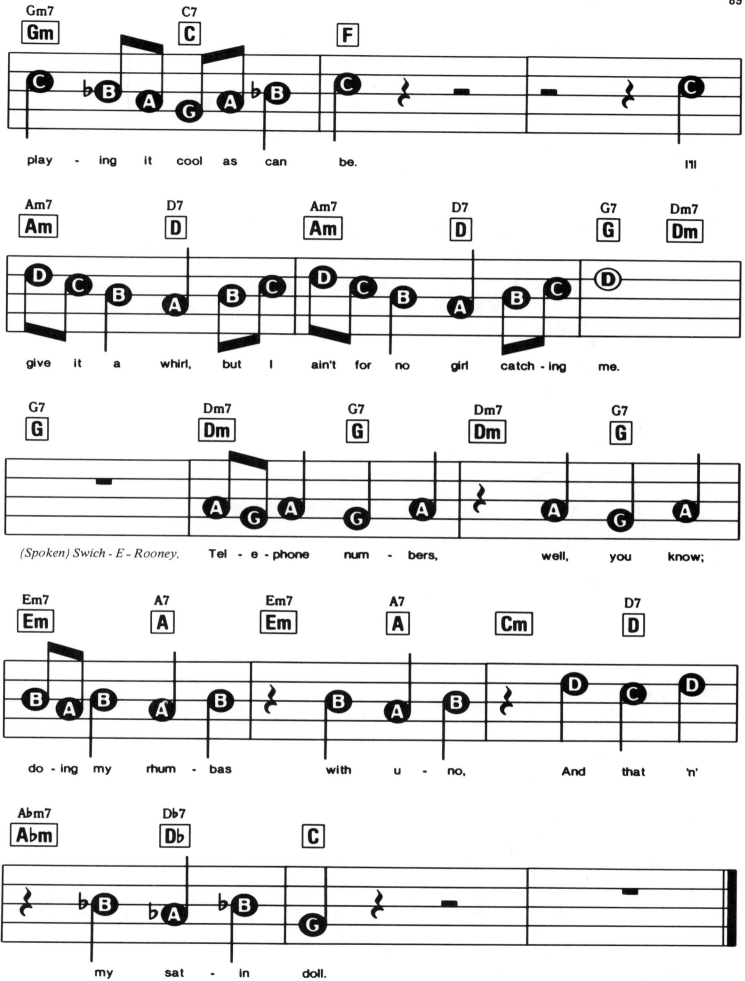

Scotch and Soda

Registration 8
Rhythm: Swing or Jazz

Words and Music by
Dave Guard

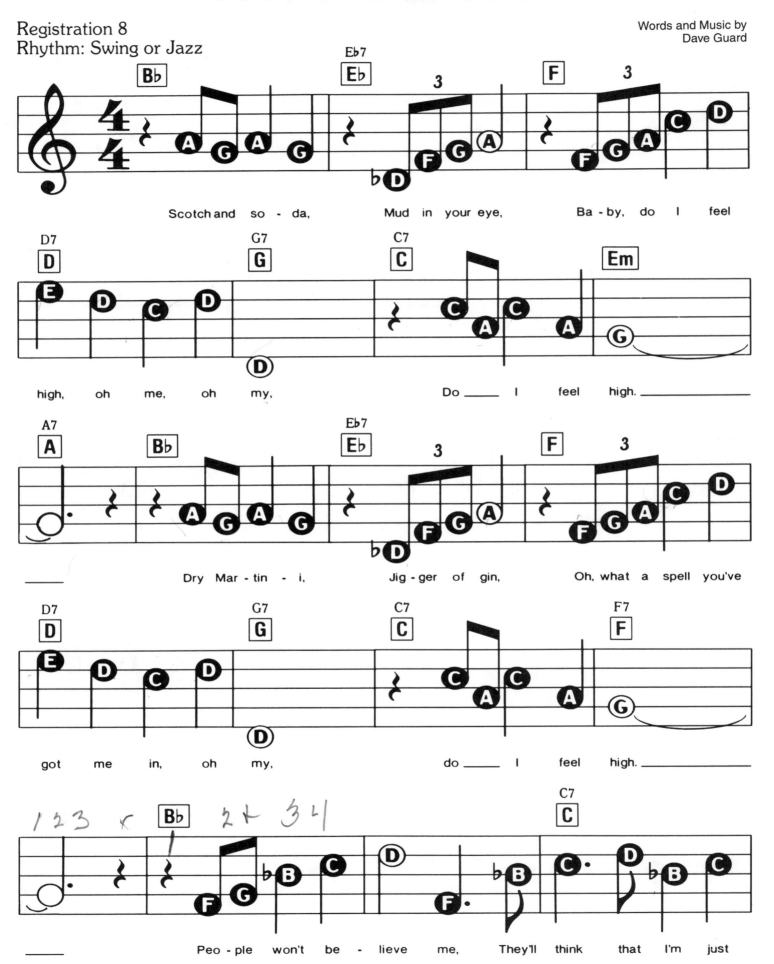

91

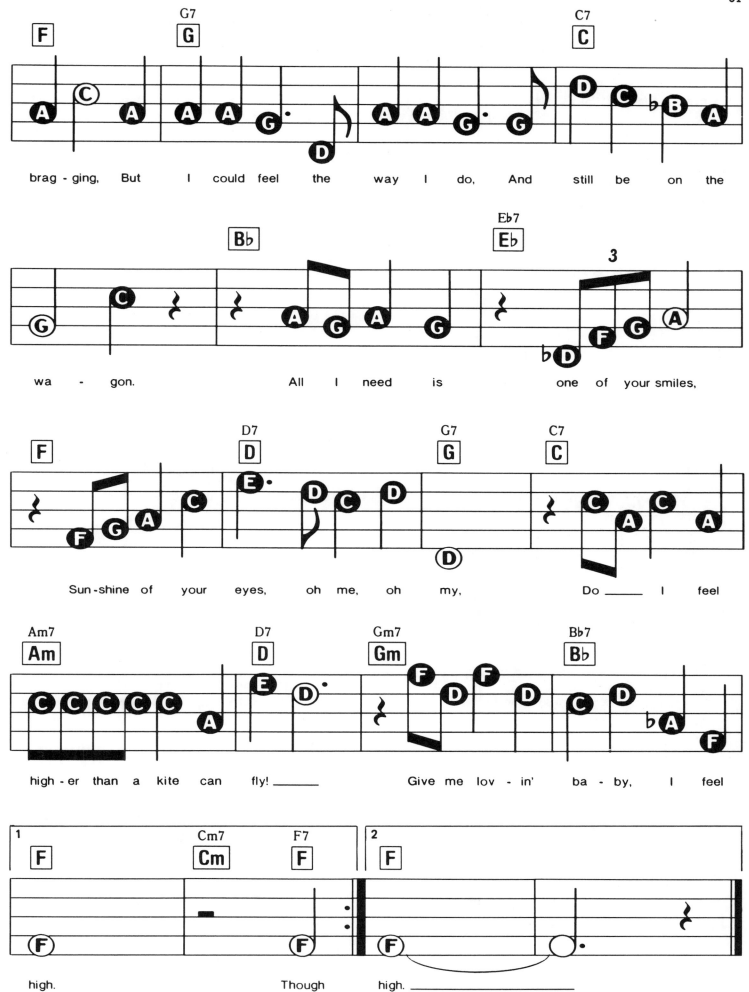

Strangers in the Night
Adapted from A MAN COULD GET KILLED

Registration 5
Rhythm: Ballad or Slow Rock

Words by Charles Singleton and Eddie Snyder
Music by Bert Kaempfert

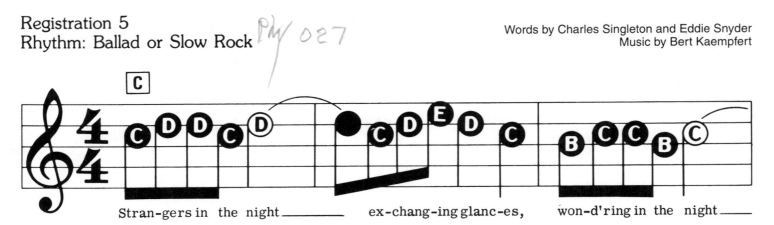

Stran-gers in the night_____ ex-chang-ing glanc-es, won-d'ring in the night _____

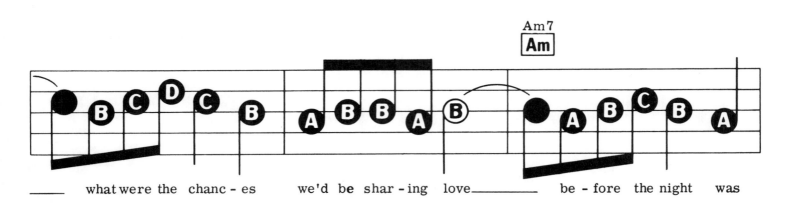

_____ what were the chanc - es we'd be shar - ing love_____ be - fore the night was

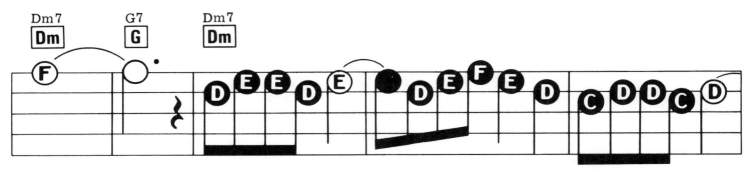

through._____ Some-thing in your eyes_____ was so in - vit - ing, Some-thing in your smile_____

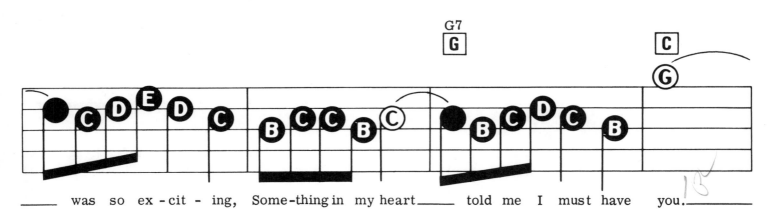

_____ was so ex - cit - ing, Some-thing in my heart_____ told me I must have you.

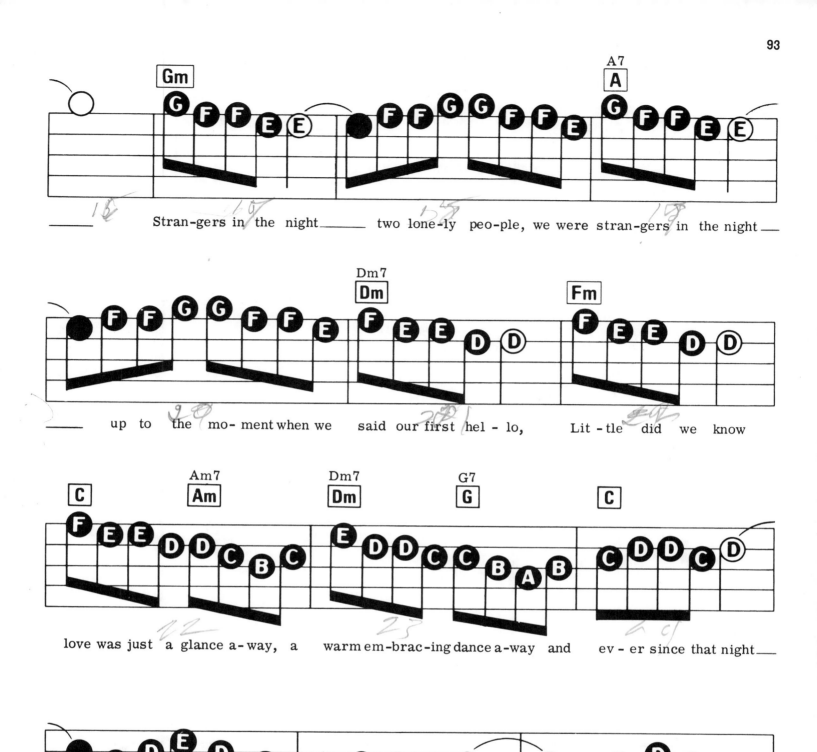

Stran-gers in the night_____ two lone-ly peo-ple, we were stran-gers in the night ____

_____ up to the mo-ment when we said our first hel - lo, Lit-tle did we know

love was just a glance a-way, a warm em-brac-ing dance a-way and ev - er since that night____

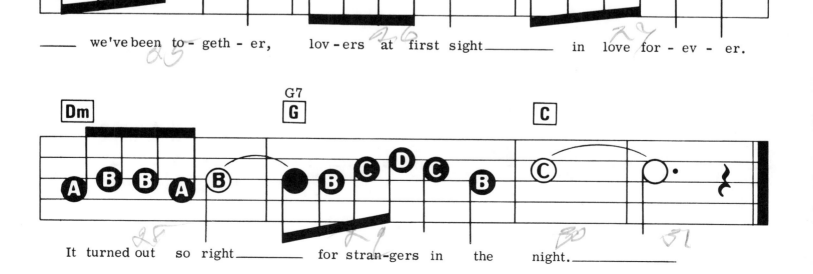

_____ we've been to - geth - er, lov-ers at first sight_____ in love for - ev - er.

It turned out so right_____ for stran-gers in the night._____

Tangerine
from the Paramount Picture THE FLEET'S IN

Registration 8
Rhythm: Swing

Words by Johnny Mercer
Music by Victor Schertzinger

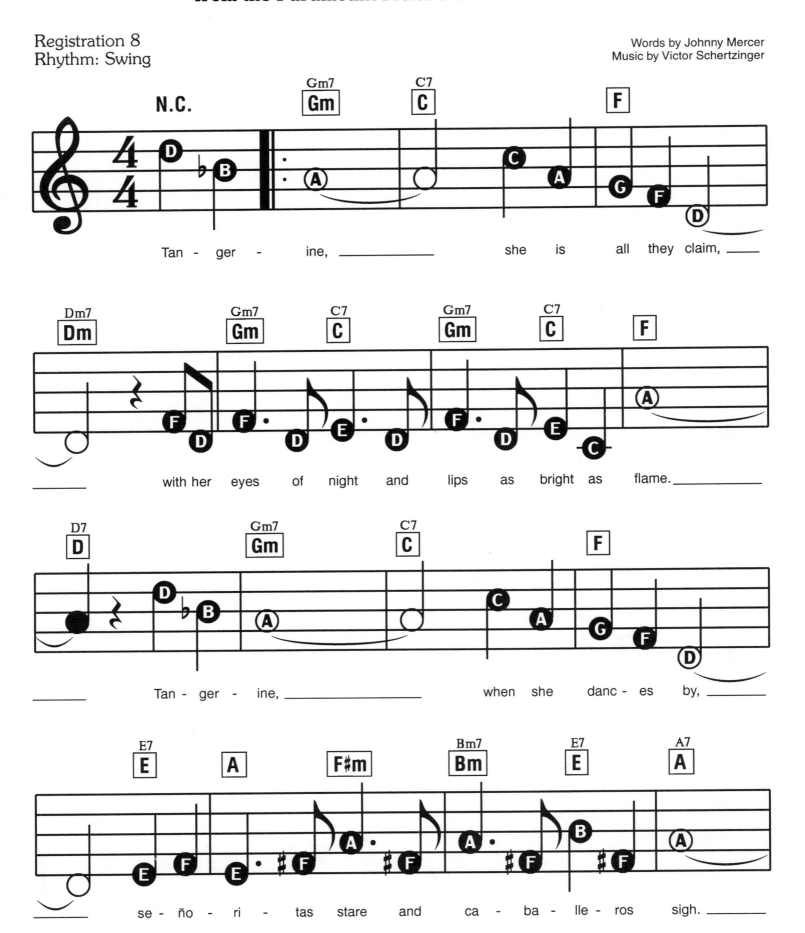

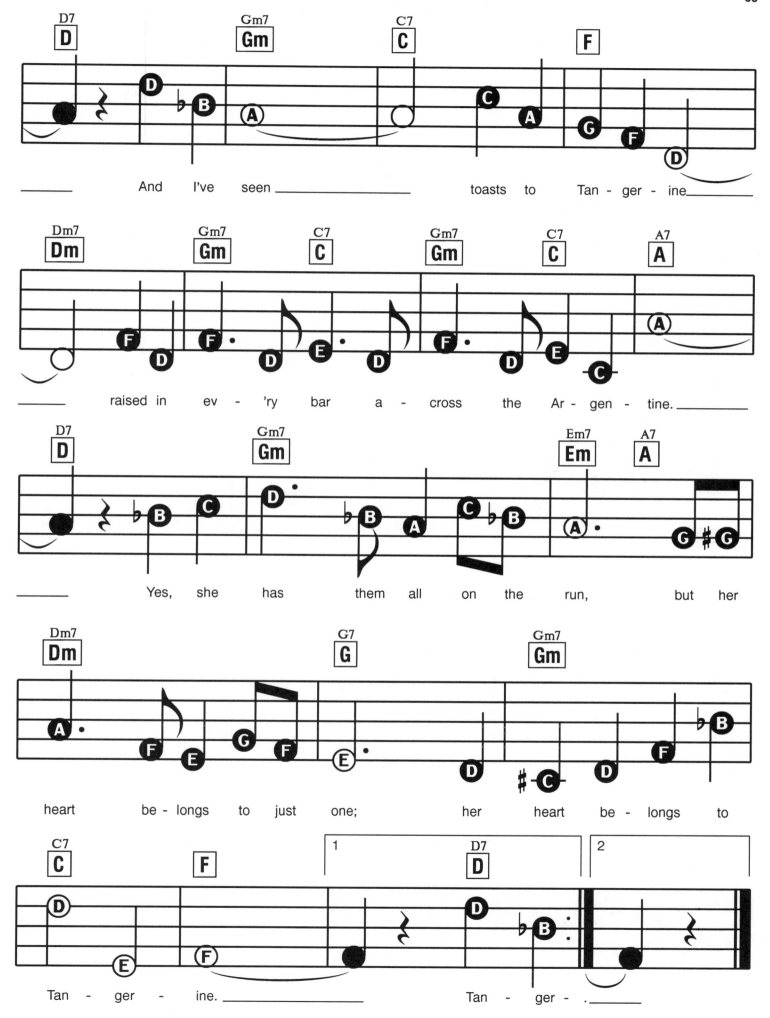

That's Life

Registration 7
Rhythm: Ballad or Swing

Words and Music by Dean Kay
and Kelly Gordon

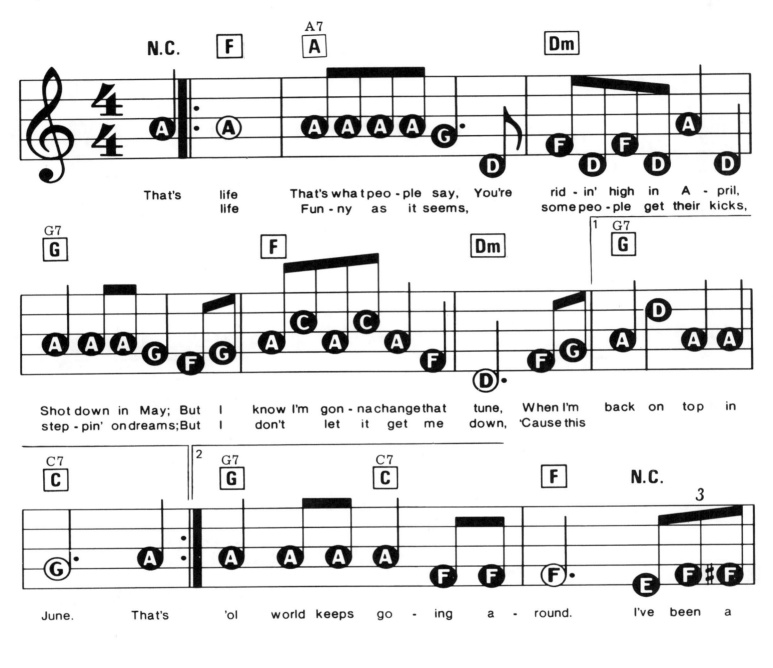

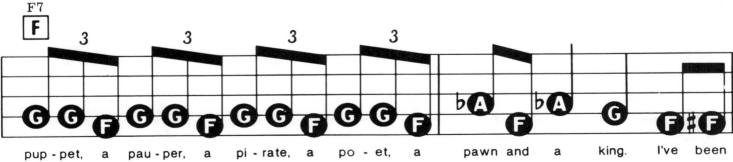

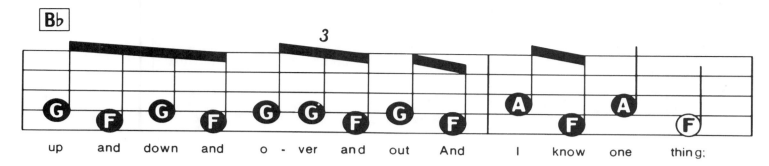

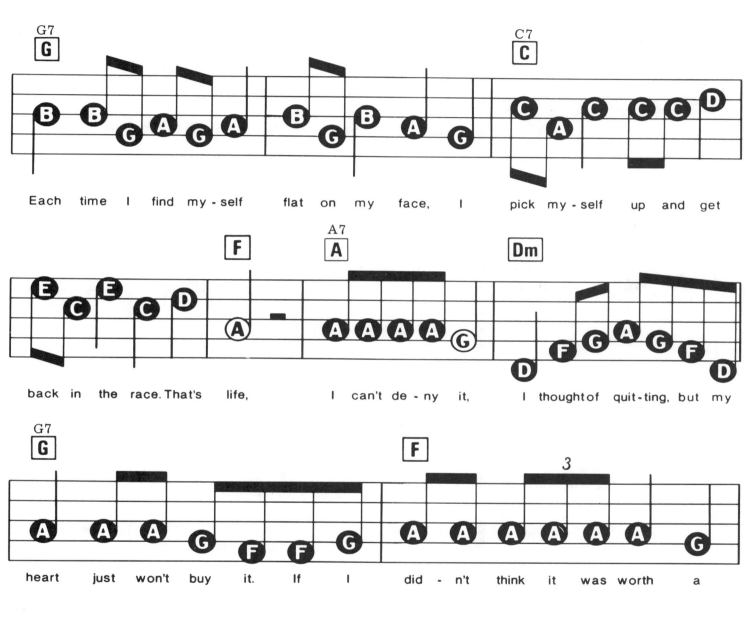

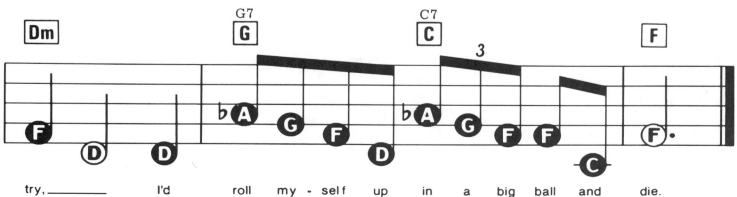

Watch What Happens

Registration 3
Rhythm: Bossa Nova or Latin
Introduction: 4 Measures

Music by Michel Legrand
Original French Text by Jacques Demy
English Lyrics by Norman Gimbel

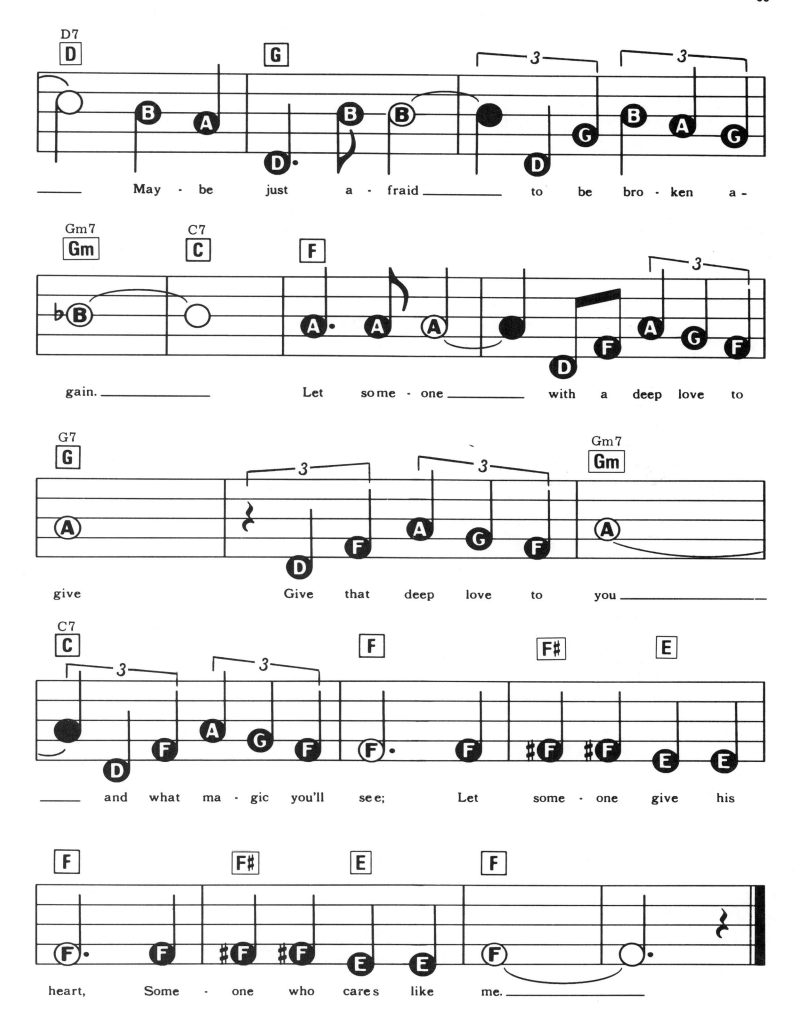

The Way We Were

Words by Alan and Marilyn Bergman
Music by Marvin Hamlisch

Registration 8
Rhythm: Slow Rock or Ballad

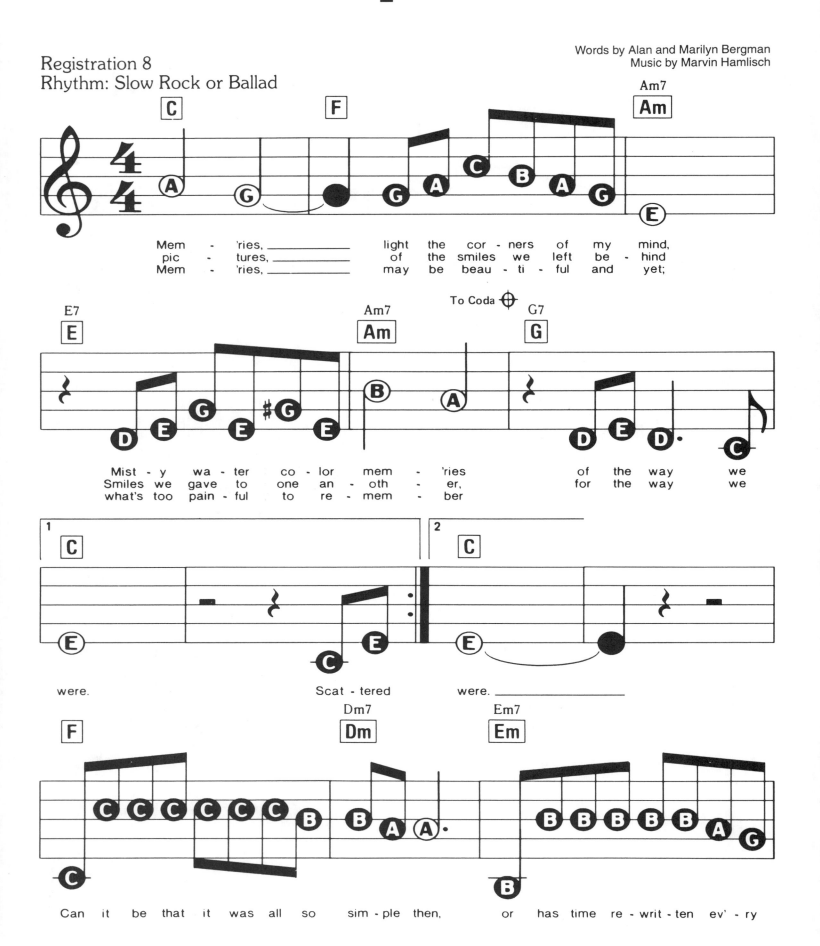

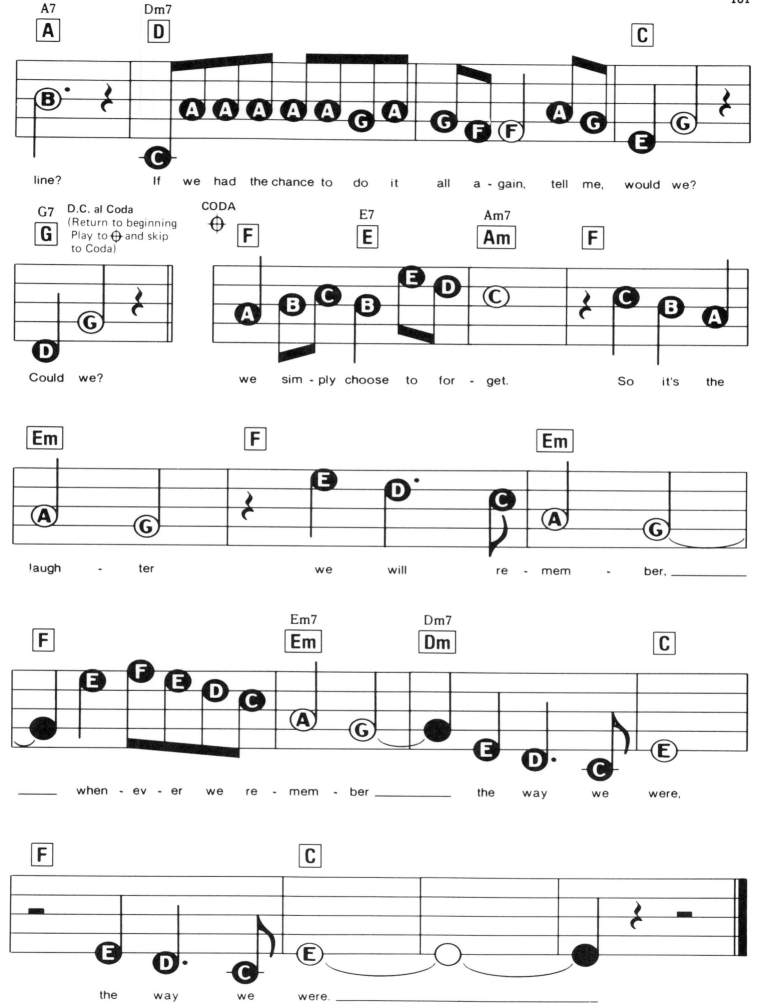

The Way You Look Tonight
from SWING TIME

Registration 3
Rhythm: Fox Trot or Swing

Words by Dorothy Fields
Music by Jerome Kern

103

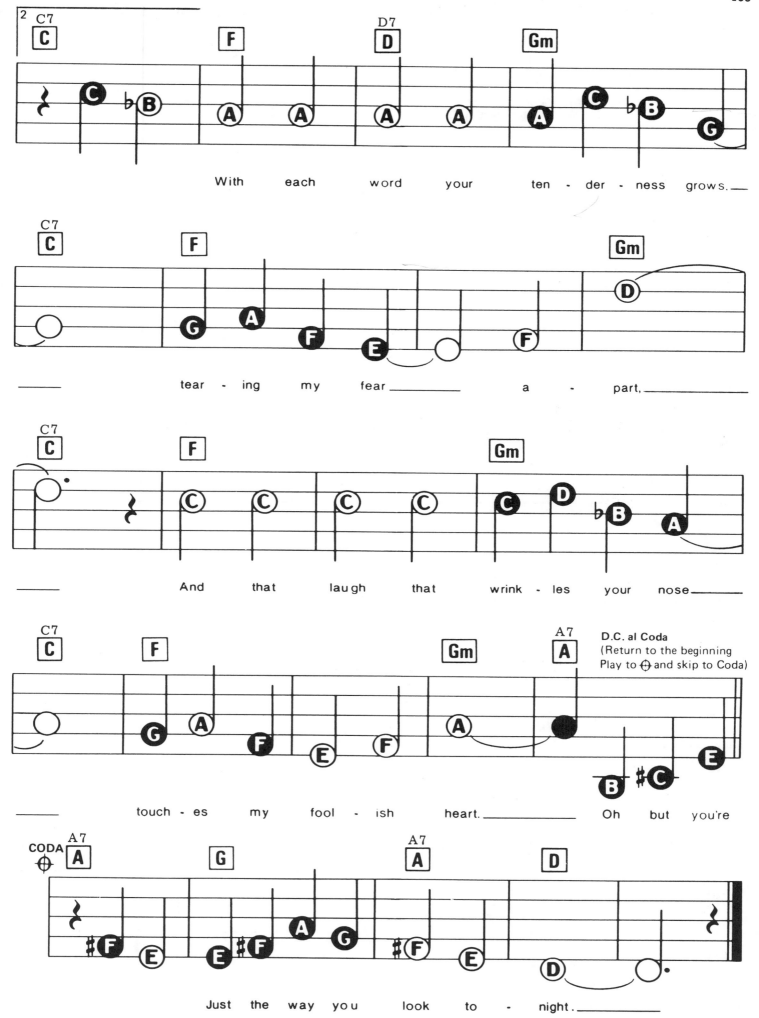

 # Registration Guide

- Match the Registration number on the song to the corresponding numbered category below. Select and activate an instrumental sound available on your instrument.

- Choose an automatic rhythm appropriate to the mood and style of the song. (Consult your Owner's Guide for proper operation of automatic rhythm features.)

- Adjust the tempo and volume controls to comfortable settings.

Registration

1	Flute, Pan Flute, Jazz Flute
2	Clarinet, Organ
3	Violin, Strings
4	Brass, Trumpet
5	Synth Ensemble, Accordion, Brass
6	Pipe Organ, Harpsichord
7	Jazz Organ, Vibraphone, Vibes, Electric Piano, Jazz Guitar
8	Piano, Electric Piano
9	Trumpet, Trombone, Clarinet, Saxophone, Oboe
10	Violin, Cello, Strings